ALSO BY TOM SERVICE

Music as Alchemy

Thomas Adès: Full of Noises

Thomas Adès: Full of Noises

Conversations with Tom Service

THOMAS ADÈS

and TOM SERVICE

Farrar, Straus and Giroux   New York

Farrar, Straus and Giroux
18 West 18th Street, New York 10011

Printed in the United States of America
Originally published in 2012 by Faber and Faber Limited, Great Britain
Published in the United States by Farrar, Straus and Giroux
First American edition, 2012

Library of Congress Cataloging-in-Publication Data
Adès, Thomas.
    Thomas Adès: full of noises : conversations with Tom Service /
Thomas Adès and Tom Service. — 1st American ed.
        p.   cm.
    Includes index.
    ISBN 978-0-374-27632-4 (hardcover : alk. paper)
    1. Adès, Thomas—Interviews.   2. Composers—England—
Interviews.   I. Service, Tom.   II. Title.

ML410.A2337A5 2012
780.92—dc23

                                                    2012024908

www.fsgbooks.com

1   3   5   7   9   10   8   6   4   2

Contents

Introduction

These conversations are full of noises in more than one sense. Most obviously, they are words about music with a constant imaginary underscore provided by the sounds, the substance and the magic of Thomas Adès's own works, as well as the music of the composers he loves and, sometimes, vehemently dislikes. They are also full of the noise of the creative friction essential to the relationship between interviewer and interviewee, especially when the latter is an artist and composer as wilfully brilliant as Adès, who is by turns thrillingly illuminating and, in the way he plays with my questions, deliberately and wittily obfuscatory. And finally, there's the white noise of the distortion that inheres in any discussion about music, obvious to a composer as naturally, dizzyingly musical as Adès: that it's his pieces themselves that provide the best answer to any question you could ask about his creativity.

But only up to a point, it turns out. These conversations do not record a forced interaction, despite Adès's famously reclusive attitude to what he's sometimes called the 'torture of public interlocution'. Rather, they are something he keenly wanted to do. For Adès, whose literary and artistic sensibilities are nearly as refined and virtuosic as his musical instincts, inhabiting the different territory of words rather than notes offers a chance to search out new creative correspondences, to open doors – a phrase he often uses – into new ways of thinking in and about music. There are new and important insights into his creative processes, glimpses of how this astonishingly musical personality hears and relates to the world, as composer, conductor and pianist; how he conjures his islands of musical invention from the sounds swirling around his head, and how he imagines and re-imagines the music of the past, from Couperin to Ligeti, Beethoven to Kurtág.

The past? There's no such thing. At least, not for Adès, whose dialogue with every composer whose music he knows, loves or loathes is as vivid and present as if they were in the room with him. Berlioz, Sibelius, Wagner, Mahler and Brahms aren't dusty personages of musical history but necessary pole stars by which Adès navigates his own musical explorations and discoveries, and they're brought to life in these discussions in the intensity of his connection with their music.

He and I have been having these kinds of conversations – in print, on the radio, on concert platforms, but mostly in private – since 2000, when I first met him for an interview for the *Guardian* about his latest piece, *America: A Prophecy*, and his then recent appointment as Artistic Director of the Aldeburgh Festival. The talking won't stop with these conversations, and the nine dialogues in this book are far from the last word on his music or any of the subjects we broach, as if such a thing were even possible. Neither are they chronological – we don't start at the beginning, with his Opus 1, the *Five Eliot Landscapes*, and end up with the opera on Luis Buñuel's film *The Exterminating Angel*, which he's writing as I'm composing these paragraphs – and nor are they exhaustive, in the sense of providing a commentary on each of his pieces.

Instead, they are conversations that are made by confronting directly and exploring indirectly, through the poetry of the unexpected tangent or allusion, the essential themes that Adès most wanted to talk about: the fine balance between stability and instability in his work, his ceaseless attempt to release what he calls the 'magnetism' between every note he writes, his desire to make his musical visions as extreme, direct, clear and moving as possible, and to return to and refine what he hears as the 'irrationally functional harmony' of Berlioz, Janáček and others. There are flashpoints on the way, because what seems as natural as breathing to Adès in how he hears the relationship of one note to another, or one harmony to the next, is something that needs explaining to the rest of us, as do his visceral loves of Beethoven, Janáček and Gerald Barry, and his equally instinctive dislikes of aspects of Wagner's music, Mahler's symphonies and Britten's operas.

But it's in the attempt to understand how Adès hears the world that these conversations will, I hope, most inspire, excite and, quite possibly, infuriate. They are, of course, metaphors for the essential experience of how Adès composes. But then, as Adès himself says, music itself is always a metaphor. The only person who knows what's really going on in that head and that imagination is Adès himself. And yet, in those moments when you hear and really connect with his music, you feel as if the world has subtly changed, as if you're seeing everything from a new perspective, through a shimmering revelatory kaleidoscope. I hope these talks can also be windows into other ways of thinking, other ways of seeing and hearing the world, musical and otherwise.

The interviews took place in Adès's London home throughout 2011, and they have been variously edited and reworked by both of us from the transcripts.

Thomas Adès: Full of Noises

I

a studio covered in scraps – stability/instability – magnetism – subjects and titles – forms and feelings – Chopin and the bottomless pool – opera and drama – absurdity – Wagner's fungus, Janáček's truth, Mahler's banality

What are you writing just now?

I'm writing something that will probably be absorbed into my new opera. I often find that smaller pieces emerge before an opera. If an idea emerges that might not go into the smaller pieces, I immediately write it on a scrap of paper and stick it to the wall. When you're writing an opera, there's so much material you might need. So anything that seems pregnant, you don't want to throw away. A scrap can stay there for years before I use it. By the end of the opera, the wall in my studio is covered with yellowing scraps.

The thing that's sitting on my desk at the moment is a piano miniature. It may become part of a larger book of miniatures, but I won't probably produce that for some time. It might be like a scrapbook, of actual thoughts that occur to one. They are a form of study – but they're sketches rather than studies exactly.

Sketches or studies in what?

I'm finding more and more that the most interesting issue is stability. That's what animates everything in music

– stability and instability. I've been asking myself: is there such a thing as absolute stability in music, or in anything? I came to the conclusion that the answer is no: where there is life, there is no stability. However, a lot of musical material – maybe all – tends to desire stability or resolution of some kind, unless it's held in a kind of equilibrium, which is still a volatile situation.

That's the way I understand everything in history, in musical history. The music we listen to is the residue of an endless search for stability. I think you can make a sort of illusion of stability in a piece; you can fix it in a certain way. In a musical work, you permanently fix something that in life would be appreciable only for a moment. The piece can stand in that relation to one's everyday experience of stability, as an ideally achieved form.

There's a contradiction there: if everything in life is unstable, that attempt at stability in a musical work is a sort of anti-life – a death.

Well, it could equally be a sort of captured, eternal volatility. You could argue that a given interval is stable, like a perfect fifth or something. But it's not, to me. The piece can be trying to resolve a tension between two ideas, to resolve them ideally into one thing. But in my case, I can hear a single note and feel all the directions it wants to move in. It might be something in the room that makes it want to move, something in the nature of the way it is played, or a quality inside me at that moment; but essentially, the note is alive and therefore unstable. If I put a note under the microscope I feel I can see millions, trillions of things. In

Polaris, my recent orchestral piece, a 'voyage for orchestra', I was looking and looking at a particular C sharp, and as I put it under the microscope I saw or heard a writhing that turned into the piece.

You talk about 'magnetism' in your programme note for Polaris: *is that a term for the pull between what's stable and what's unstable in your music?*

That's really what one is dealing with all the time, magnetism: understanding the magnetic pull of the notes put in a given disposition, their shifting relative weights. I have a problem – well, it's not a problem for me, but it can make life confusing talking to anyone else – which is that I don't believe at all in the official distinction between tonal and atonal music. I think the only way to understand these things is that they are the result of magnetic forces within the notes, which create a magnetic tension, an attraction or repulsion. The two notes in an interval, or any number of chords, have a magnetic relationship of attraction or repulsion which creates movement in one direction or another. A composer, whether of a symphony or a pop song, is arranging these magnetic objects in a certain disposition. That means that sometimes, in order to understand the weight of one note and the next note to it, you might have to transfer meaning from one to another. In *Polaris*, I had to transfer meaning from the C sharp to the A in order to do that. And it was difficult in some ways, because to really discover what the notes want to do, you might have to go against what they at first appear to want to do, and then they start to resist and you have to use other magnets to see what they are really feeling.

Is that a pre-compositional idea in Polaris, *that decision to look at that C sharp, to work out what that move from C sharp to A meant?*

There's no such thing as 'pre-composition': as soon as you start you're really composing. I wouldn't distinguish between a 'pre-compositional' and a 'during-composition' stage. What if you have to go back to the 'pre-compositional stage', which would almost certainly happen? You're dealing with something that is chronically volatile. It's like lava, except my material doesn't actually exist in physical reality. They are evanescent sounds. These notes are not objects that are in front of you – although in another sense it helps to treat them like that; maybe they are, in fact, a sort of invisible object. But that very invisibility is frustrating, because one's brain can't necessarily define them clearly at first.

That idea of 'where the notes want to go', their magnetic weights relative to one another – I can hear a lot of your music in those terms when you put it like that.

Any music. It's the way I hear.

That's different from other living composers.

Good!

Is Polaris *doing something very different from what your music has always done?*

I think working with magnets is what I was always doing. I perhaps felt in the past that it wouldn't be interesting enough on its own to make a piece out of, that it would be more interesting to have a descriptive subject for the piece. When I was younger, it was helpful, in some ways, to have a subject; it was a short cut to the point where things are sitting in a permanent equilibrium, a resolution, even if it's an uncomfortable one.

Is it when you sense a permanent equilibrium that you feel a piece is finished?

It can be. A piece can have more than one ending. My first opera, *Powder Her Face*, has three or four endings; different surfaces, different keys in it that end at different points. And that comes from the nature of the subject; there are different layers. And my orchestral piece *Asyla* has a couple of endings, some in a row and then some on top of each other – I can't remember how many. When they are all in place I can sense the equilibrium. It is quite exciting to find all those resolutions happening at once.

How do you choose the subject of a piece, and once chosen, does it risk limiting the piece? How and why do you choose a descriptive title, like Asyla, *or an abstract, generic title, as in your Piano Quintet?*

Well, all pieces have subjects, whether stated in the title or not. That was another problem for me: I don't see the distinction between abstract music and programme music. I literally have no idea what that means, because to me all music is metaphorical, always. That textbook distinction is meaningless to me. Also, to me abstract titles are difficult to use without sounding pretentious or in bad taste. I find 'symphony' impossible to use now: it sounds so affected. I think, though, one would still be able to use the word 'symphony' in the sense that Purcell does, meaning instrumental music at the beginning of a masque or something; that makes perfect sense to me.

So you feel the subject, the title, used to be a way in to the music for you, which now you need less?

I can now access more immediately the metaphorical implications of a note or two notes, without the need for an image or a picture, whereas in the past, the metaphorical freight was expressed in a title or an idea. It doesn't bother me much either way; it's a natural, musical process.

There is a distinction you're talking about, though: when you are 'just' combining notes, with no further subject, is the freight of metaphors different, less heavy?

It's completely indistinguishable, whether one names the subject behind a musical idea or chooses not to. I might not be able to name it. I might try very hard and not come up with a name. In my piano piece *Traced Overhead* I had about a hundred and fifty titles for it before I came to that one. I almost called it 'Sonata da Sopra'. I can't explain why that wasn't logical enough. It's not ultimately up to me, whether I reject one avenue and choose another one. It is very like walking blind: you run into an obstacle and you go the other way. Or perhaps you try to do something with the obstacle. Whatever it is that leads you to reject one path – even if it's something larger, a whole section that you do or don't write, or a detail that you choose over another – all of those choices are made at a level that's almost completely instinctive and emotional. But I find that there is almost always an analytical reason behind those decisions, which suddenly becomes clear at the last minute, when I've finished the composition, and I see: oh, this melody was the inversion of that one, or there was some other technical connection, all along.

So is all this a conscious or subconscious thing?

As I said, it's the same thing either way: when I say analytical, it's because you sense this form internally and have to find a way to realise it. And that is an analytical process – whether conscious or not makes no difference. Usually it's not explicitly conscious at the start. It may be like seeing the face in the fire, which isn't actually there, but once you've written it down, it becomes real. Just as if an artist draws a face they see in the fire, then once it is drawn that face becomes a real face. Writing music is like trying to draw the face in the fire.

That's fine in principle, but there are moments in your music where there are conscious uses of forms: chaconnes, say. Surely these are decisions that aren't so instinctive: I mean, if you're writing a chaconne, you must have made a decision to write a chaconne?

No! That's not true. This is a very common mistake. That's not how one makes a decision. That is what is wrong with academic analysis. The impulse comes first, the method second. The desire to travel faster preceded the invention of the car. It was desire that generated the design. A chaconne is simply one kind of harmonic motion. In my music it's very often spiral rather than circular – in other words, it's transposed down with each appearance, or whatever it is. But it's really an organic form, a kind of growth, and the label 'chaconne' comes after. The same goes for 'sonata form' or 'fugue'. It's not to say 'I'm going to do that because composer X did it'– I wouldn't think like that, really. I mean, some do, of course, but I think the duty should be first to the desire of the material, second to the formal plan, otherwise it remains like a photograph, faded. But there may already be something in the nature of the material that tends towards a particular form – in which case it's not really referential in that sense. I mean, again, everything is metaphorical in music.

Maybe a chaconne, or any formal structure, is something that helps you feel less blind when you're composing, and you perhaps see the obstacles more clearly, before you run into them?

Well, in some ways, perhaps. But you could say that any serial piece is a chaconne of a kind, in the sense that you're going through rotations of the twelve notes of the row in order. You could describe the whole serial process as a chaconne if you felt like it, but it's really just to do with the way that notes recur. And if they happen to recur in a certain recognisable way – suddenly the piece is a chaconne. What I'm saying is: the distance between something that's a repetitive structure in that explicit sense, and the way a continually unfolding structure – like the first movement of *Asyla*, say – actually works, is quite small. I might have set out to write that as a chaconne, but the material didn't allow it.

I began that piece, *Asyla*, by writing the melody, in fact, where the horns enter. And then in the course of completing that melody, I found that I had to start to compose the harmonisation at the same time in order to understand how the melody was moving. And then the accompaniment, the harmonisation, began to take on a life of its own, and at that point I couldn't make it into a chaconne. It had already run somewhere else, and I had to let it do what it wanted. There is quite a long development of the melody, and you could almost see it as a chaconne, yet it's not. It doesn't sound like one – but it's much more closely related to one than you might think, and it does have a spiral form. And then I had to compose an introduction to the first movement later, and then the middle section is based on Couperin. And then it's simply a recapitulation. So it's never very far from classical form, really.

You make it sound as if all that just happened without any intervention from you, as if there were scarcely any decisions to be made about what to do with the material. But you must surely have been shaping it, grappling with it, all the time. I mean: take that melody in the first movement of Asyla, *for example: where does it lie in relation to the question of stability and instability?*

I'm afraid in that case it can be a sort of Chinese box effect. That is: I answer one instability with another, and it can resemble a hall of mirrors. There are models for this. Take Chopin – one knows that there must be a point of possible resolution somewhere in his music, partly because it's the nineteenth century; but mostly, there is nothing stable. As soon he puts a note on the page it starts to slide around. And there is no real resolution. It's like a pool you can't see the bottom of. You're aware of the movement of the water, and there may be currents of different temperatures that affect one another, and indeed there must be a bottom to it, but you can't necessarily see it. In fact, if Chopin gives you a resolution, it's a concession on his part, a concession to us. The music doesn't really demand it.

Or you could have a Beethovenian model, which is in the other direction most of the time, yet it's actually quite similar. What I mean is it's more volcanic: in Beethoven, the bottom can simply move under your feet. That's what catalyses his music. That's a different world, but as models of ways to think about the question of stability, they're quite good twin ideas.

Are you aware of the bottom of the pool when writing your own music?

As much as any swimmer is. But sometimes one is in the deep ocean. That's one of the interesting things about doing something on an operatic scale. The distance is too great from one shore to the other; but you have to approach it in the same way as you articulate the drama of a piano piece, with tonality, the magnetic forces of notes.

You will find as an opera goes on that because of the demands the drama makes on the music, there will emerge relations between tonalities, or centres of magnetic polarity, whatever you want to call them, and that will affect the resolution, indeed the ending. There will be some quite clear symmetry or geometry in the relations, but it will be unlikely to begin and end in the same key, because something in the course of the opera will have caused the ground beneath us to shift. There will always be some unfolding process in any piece, but in an opera it could go anywhere, because instead of having two or three or four layers of desire, as you might have in a piano piece, there might be, say, fifteen, and that creates much more slippage. You might have so many, in fact, that you're not sure who, if you like, is going to win. I know what happens to the characters on stage in the story, but I don't know how that functions in the music until it's composed.

In my second opera, *The Tempest*, the resolution comes about through renunciation. The characters depart and leave the island. The music resolved in a key that was somewhat unexpected but it arrived with so much force that it was clearly the right thing. But I hadn't foreseen it. The music finds D flat and stays there right to the end. This is a new key in the piece, although the third act opens with a premonition of it. That's because you have a situation at the end of the piece which has not happened in the drama before. You have two characters who have never been on stage at the same time – alone, with everyone else gone. There is peace, natural peace: harmony between Caliban, representing the island, because he is at last its king, and Ariel, who has been set free and is now simply the air, and the sea. So you could say that the stability is something that is always present in the opera, but which is revealed only at the end.

In The Tempest, *with all those materials moving in different directions – if the notes have their own will, do the individual characters have will too?*

Well, the characters don't exist without the material: when I say characters I'm talking about fifteen separate tendencies in the material, which are more or less related.

But I mean, you have events that have to happen in the story, so . . .

Well, I have to create those events using my notes.

Is that different from writing instrumental music, where you can follow the will of the notes without inhibition, as opposed to an opera, where you know you have events coming up in the drama that will demand a certain type of music?

No – it's similar. You're more powerfully aware in opera of swimming from one sort of pole to another, but the poles become very important to one another. As Morton Feldman says about Beethoven: it's not so much how he gets into things that's interesting, it's how he gets out of them. That's very good. And an opera is really about getting out of things, that's what it is. You get these people in this situation and then: oh God, how are we going to get out of this? The notes have to do that too. How are we going to get off stage? How are we going to get *home*?

What is the principal difference between writing an opera and writing something else?

Well obviously it takes more time, it's longer. Aside from that there's the question of the scale of the gestures. There is a mysterious thing that happens when you set actions to music: a third shape that emerges when something non-visual like a musical score is acted out by people moving on a stage. You know, to make this completely absurd thing watchable in any way, it's not that straightforward. There's no absolute way to do it. You just have to do it instinctively or not at all. Most of the time I sit there and watch operas and think: this is all absurd. Really we shouldn't all be here!

Are you trying to get past that?

No, that is the point, the more absurd, the more indefensible, the more it makes sense! Operas that are worthily about something, some idea or ideal, and that try to make a point, especially a political point, are just absurd in a bad way, in an off-putting way. Operas should instead be absurd in a way that is truer than reality. But that's just the most absurd form of something that is absurd from the start: music. Music should have no excuse, other than itself. Music is its own excuse.

So concerts are absurd too?

Oh, completely. What are we doing here? What are all those musicians doing? More so in opera, because you have this further absurdity of the supposed psychology of the characters on stage. I really want to do something where their psychology is not the important point. Because you can't just believe that these characters have a psychology of their own unless it is genuinely, unequivocally encoded in the music. Psychological problems in themselves are not really a strong enough force for musical structure. This is the root of my problem with Wagner.

But it's the opposite of a composer like Janáček, whom I love. In *Jenůfa*, for example, the wicked stepmother throws the baby in the lake. And when this is discovered there is a huge reaction from the chorus. That's absurd because there is no baby and there is no lake. But they have to have that reaction because there is a seismic harmonic event which creates the baby in the lake, and their reaction follows. The lighting and the direction have to follow the harmony too – to do what the music tells it, not the drama. Otherwise it's boring.

Can you expand on that? What about the power of Wagner's music to cause seismic events in something like Tristan und Isolde?

Well, I find that much less interesting than Janáček's operas about fate, in a way – because I think music in an opera should be a sort of fate that the characters are going to be subjected to.

But isn't that exactly what Tristan *is about?*

No! Because they're taking drugs, aren't they? It's artificial. They're not really that keen on each other. I can hear that in the music, it's inorganic.

But the music in Tristan – *that's surely the fate that drives them, that they can't escape from?*

Really . . .

. . . I mean the whole thing is about an unstable situation from bar one which ends up in an image of stability which the whole thing is striving for and reaches only at the end of the piece – it's a place that they're all trapped in until the very end.

I don't know, I find it a bit too long.

I'm not defending it, necessarily, in those terms, but surely in Wagner the fate of the characters is in the music. Why doesn't Wagner do that for you?

It's too psychological. I'm thinking of *The Ring* more than *Tristan*, there's an awful lot of psychology in it which I find tedious. And naive, in a sort of superficial, German way. I mean, so much of *Parsifal* is dramatically absurd, which would be fine if the music was aware of the absurdity, but it is as if the whole piece is drugged and we all have to pretend that it's not entirely ridiculous. And it seems to me that a country that can take something as funny as Kundry seriously, this woman who sleeps for aeons and is only woken up by this horrible chord, a country that can seriously believe in anything like *Parsifal* without laughing, was bound to get into serious trouble.

You're obviously not convinced by the music?

I don't find Wagner's an organic, necessary art. Wagner's music is fungal. I think Wagner is a fungus. It's a sort of unnatural growth. It's parasitic in a sense – on its models, on its material. His material doesn't grow symphonically – it doesn't grow through a musical logic – it grows parasitically. It has a laboratory atmosphere.

What does it grow through, then?

It grows through an unhealthy perversion of early German mediaeval fairy tales and myth, which are wonderful things, you know, in their original forms. But in my view they need to be treated lightly, on the wing, rather than in this grotesquely inflated, bombastic, off-putting way. Admittedly if you take a few slices of fungus or of Wagner, perhaps ten or fifteen minutes, it's magnificent, you can't fault it. In fact you could say: quite clearly this is the best music of its time, perhaps he's even the best, most masterly composer ever. But when you put it together, one slice after another, it seems to me to have a sort of undead quality, a vampiric quality, because he animates these dramas by slices of marvellous music, but they don't build into something real. Wagner is a Golem.

People talk about them as symphonic operas, though, and celebrate them in exactly those terms, because of their fusion of 'symphonic' thinking with music theatre, creating his music dramas.

I think that's just because they don't have proper numbers, but that's just a kind of incompetence. He's quite weak on articulating an actual section of music. The reason is that Wagner is not interested in releasing the inherent, organic power – what I would mean by genuinely 'symphonic' power – of his (often magnificent) cells. It's just a pose. Good symphonies are often in some ways an unfolding sequence of miniatures. They have to go through miniature forms as they go along, and what bothers me with Wagner's music is that there's a pretence of some kind of symphonic thought where there actually isn't any, where none is possible because he can't trust himself. Instead, you just have these people – or elves or gods or whatever they are – marching about the stage and whacking each other with sticks. Berlioz, in *Les Troyens*, is much more successful to me. In that opera, you are clear that there are numbers, that there are actors in a drama, and that something is happening: obviously we're not actually in 1000 BC Troy, but we are taking part in a symphonic event in which specific things are happening and they are woven into a music which is in itself dramatically alive. The drama becomes more real because the artifice is more transparent.

The Wagnerian project was an attempt to get closer to psychological or emotional 'truth', by dissolving artifice, by dissolving the numbers – arias, choruses, duets – of earlier operatic traditions. The image you used for Chopin is like what happens in Wagner's music, surely, because you're swimming around in a pool where you don't know if there's a bottom.

Not at all: Chopin's pieces are exquisitely balanced – he will always begin it and finish it. The water is completely clear. For sure, you feel that you're in some endless vortex of some kind, but they are very definitely symphonic because there's a logic from the first note to the last, you just may not be able to parse exactly what the logic is. But in Wagner the logic is philosophical or psychological. It's not a musical logic. The water is murky. It's filthy. That's why it's like fungus. You see, to me, notes are like angels, they are innocent at the point of origin. But the moment Wagner writes a note it is forced to stand for something extra-musical. The metaphor is not a musical one.

But you say all music is metaphorical.

Yes, but not political. In Wagner every note is political and that to me is repulsive. Ethics are a distraction an artist cannot afford.

Every note in Wagner political? Is that unique to him?

He can't seem to help it. Wagner's notes seem to come into the world with badges on: 'I mean this, I mean that. I represent this issue, I broach that subject.' They are born wearing little uniforms. Or perhaps I should say, insignia. That's one of the reasons directors and writers can't leave his operas alone. It's catnip for them: wall-to-wall issues.

Yet you play the 'Prelude and Liebestod' from Tristan *in Liszt's piano arrangement?*

But I told you, Wagner does write wonderful slices, and of course Liszt is a much more interesting composer, although he was very disturbed by Wagner, in lots of ways, as was everybody. But Liszt disturbed Wagner even more. All the techniques of harmonic movement, the great inventions in Wagner, were actually invented by Liszt. Liszt's *Faust Symphony* made *Tristan* possible – I'm talking in strictly harmonic terms. Without it *Tristan* would not have been possible.

Are you disturbed by the human side of Wagner?

I don't know anything about that. I really don't. I'm sure I would be, but I'm not interested. There are such magnificent heights of invention in his music, but I like very much something Proust wrote about the effort involved in getting there (and Proust was a fan): he wrote that at such heights, one had to expect a certain amount of engine noise.

When I talk about Wagner's 'fungal' quality, by the way, I'm talking about something quite technical: his music isn't a tree, it's a fungus.

Whereas Janáček, by contrast, is a fully organic tree?

Yes, Janáček's music is organic – a flower that blooms, because the sap of the feeling in the music is there from the very beginning and that's what drives it, rather than some creepy philosophical agenda. Janáček's response to what is happening in the drama is so direct in the music: I think there's nothing but response and music in it. There's nothing external. You don't have to wait in Janáček for things to happen, as you do in Wagner, while he does something seductive for half an hour.

So when you are watching an opera, you want to feel that there are organic things in the music that are driving everything along? But what if the story is one of violent disruption?

This can be misunderstood: when I say 'organic', I don't exclude violent dislocations. The dislocations are just as much part of the organic process. It's like pruning a tree. You often have to cut to preserve the life of the plant. That's like what Janáček does: in his operas, a process peremptorily stops dead yet the energy is still transferred to what happens next in some mysterious way. That could be what gives the music its power, those cuts and hard juxtapositions. That's organic too. There's no contradiction. Every idea is presented with its maximum force. That seems to me more completely evolved, more arrived, than in any nineteenth-century opera, except *Les Troyens*.

I'm analytically interested in the piano music of Janáček, because you see a move there from the early works, which are quite close to Schumann's pieces, basically binary in form, rather predictable in a way. Like Schumann, they're sweet, but not quite professional in a way –

Hold on – Schumann's aren't professional?

They're not really on the level of Chopin or somebody. They just seem like someone a little bit academic in his thinking, as opposed to a professional composer – but that's a digression – back to Janáček ... In his next pieces, like *Along an Overgrown Path*, Janáček will refract things, very simply, by a knight's move in the harmony. What that creates is a sort of dislocation, a shuttering in the structural image, that is very like putting a pencil in the water: instead of seeing a straight line, you see a line moving across in waves and ripples. And with that you step into the moment, you step into his moment. It becomes very real, it becomes the present tense of your actual experience. It's a magical effect.

The more I think about the title of that piece, *Along an Overgrown Path*, I realise that it's a Proustian thing. Janáček wants to recapture the distant past, which is no longer there, the moment has vanished. But, once, the path was not overgrown. The music is the memories, which are still alive. It's the same with *In the Mists*: that is a very exciting structure. All of Janáček's pieces are, really. In a way you could look at them and say they are all just ABA ABCA ABACA, very simple binary or tertiary structures.

But you realise with Janáček that when he says something twice it's immediately different the second time, because of where it is in the structure. You feel that time has passed. There may even have been a modulation that makes the tonic feel like a memory. And I think that's why, in Janáček's operas, his characters move through time in the music. There's nothing in his music that's pretending to create an external form: what the music is doing is taking the moment you're listening to and making that the exact same moment it would have been when he was listening to it. So you perceive the reality of time: that it's vertical rather than horizontal and you can look down into the past.

I said before that one often tends to create an illusion of stability in a piece that leads to the end. But in Janáček, this can work the other way round. He'll take one moment, and show you the inner instability in that moment, and then hold that as a sort of frozen moment of emotion, of pain or apprehension, and freeze it in time. And the ramifications of several of those moments placed next to one another are then only revealed on the last page. In that piece, *In the Mists*, nothing changes, but you're aware that every time the silence comes back, and he tries another doorway, it transforms from being a phenomenon that opens a new possibility to something that closes the structure. Yet the material doesn't change. There's no rhetoric in a way. So thereby Janáček rediscovers a kind of classical purity. Haydn can do that, and Beethoven can do that, but it's a thing that was almost lost in the middle of the nineteenth century. There was that attempt to create an illusion of revelation and redemption through music that possibly diverted something quite fundamental about what we're doing when we write a note.

You mean the move in the Austro-German works of the nineteenth century towards making music enact a form of redemption, and thereby create a sort of transcendent metaphysics: that whole project, in your terms, comes at the expense of something essential in the musical material, meaning that it no longer has an existence as an object in itself?

Well, no: some marvellous music, some of the greatest, like Beethoven's Ninth, for goodness' sake, is a form of composed redemptive action. But later, perhaps when the redemption becomes more enacted than actually composed, that's the moment when one wants to step back. It's simply less interesting to me. That's why, say, a Mahler symphony can be so embarrassing. Because he's so keen to make whatever his point is that you sometimes wonder whether he's stopped being interested in what he's actually putting on paper. Put it like this: there's an embarrassment between the job the music's being asked to do and its qualifications for doing that job. The material is so relentlessly banal that it must be deliberate. There is almost no really good, original material in Mahler. There's a huge amount of cheap, automatic trash – I'm talking very specifically about the material, the melodies, the images.

You're talking about the street music, the popular tunes?

The problem is bad faith, because Mahler is quite clearly a composer of the utmost sophistication. One only has to look at the songs. It is almost as though he holds his own talent so cheap that there is a kind of self-loathing, as if by expressing himself in the grandest symphonic context using melodies that are the musical equivalent of street food, hot dogs, pretzels, he will avoid saying something too weighty, almost. He gets round it by being doggedly sarcastic, by which I mean brilliant orchestration, intense staging, dazzling effects of perspective, but really there's an evasiveness there.

It's hard to use material like that convincingly in concert music: trashy material. Someone like Poulenc I think succeeds, but there isn't such a distance there between the artist and the source as one feels in Mahler. But for me the most successful example is the barrel-organ music in the final scene of *Lulu*: it is at once something literally external, heard outside the window in the street in King's Cross, and outside the serial environment that we are living in, but at the same time woven entirely into the web so that it belongs to the supremely intricate universe Berg has created. There is a total unity between the highest and lowest material.

You resist the idea of a resurrection in music, or of hymns for the whole world, those sorts of ideas in Mahler's symphonies?

The subject-matter is a decoy to distract from the banality of the material. The Eighth Symphony particularly is terribly weak. God knows what it's supposed to be about – Jesus, Faust, some nonsense. That's an embarrassing piece. It's as though one's seeing him naked in public. And he looks like a phoney. But then, on the other hand, when he embraces and celebrates the futility of his life and his music, it's much more successful, for me. The Sixth Symphony, *Das Lied von der Erde*, and especially the Ninth Symphony. Because his material suits futility.

The Ninth Symphony is really the beginning of something, for me. As well as being the end, for him. The rest of Mahler seems like a preparation for it. He finally stops evading.

Isn't the embarrassment rather more like seeing the vanity of his compositional ambition naked, not him, in the Eighth symphony?

What's the difference? It's exposing to see the compositional vanity not working. But – in another way – good for him.

Grand failures are preferable to sneaky successes, aren't they? It may be just a national characteristic of mine. In England we tend not to accept things at face value. We have a very highly developed nose for phoniness. We won't just accept something as sublime or whatever just because it tells us it is. But it's also very British of me to blame myself for being embarrassed at someone else's ludicrousness.

the impossibility of repetition – musical promiscuity in
Powder Her Face *– In Seven Days and religious feeling –*
the fifth and the fourth as intervals and ideas – Asyla *and*
César Franck – Verdi's brainlessness – cliché and kitsch –
musical conveyances – the finale problem – ending and
freefalling

Would you agree that a lot of your music seems to be permanently in flux?

I don't believe in stability, I don't think it exists, in life. At least, it seems to want its own destruction, just as instability wants resolution. The moment I put a note down on paper it starts to slide around on the page. And the writhing that I could see when I look at a note under the microscope, you would see with any living thing.

It's the opposite of exact repetition – yet there is more repetitive material in your recent music. Has your attitude to repetition changed?

Often people aren't aware that music is in motion in front of them all the time, that with each note it's either closer or further away, it's not in the same place that it was before. It can't be. If you play one note twice, it's going to have different implications, because you will have been altered by the first one.

I don't really think exact repetition is possible, especially in performance: it's simply a different kind of movement. I'm talking about what happens when a musical image moves through time, because you've got a little older than when it was first played, and you've probably started to think about something more, as we do when we get older. So the second time it comes, it has more urgency.

Are there other things that you're doing now which you consciously avoided in your earlier work?

I think I was – I couldn't help myself – being happily promiscuous with pre-existing music. I was that age. It's completely pretentious to imagine that you can do without other music, 'found' things perhaps, especially at the age of twenty or twenty-five. By the way, I don't think of references as 'found' things, more as 'keepings' – that was Gerard Manley Hopkins' word: things that are already in one's cupboard but which you don't bother to throw out, because there's still some use in them and there's no moral reason to throw something away when it still has use.

Now, I sensed the dangers of that, for the reality of the pieces I was writing. The 'kept' music had to seem part of my piece, rather than merely an ironic or even a sarcastic distraction. It wasn't a joke. I wasn't joking, you see. And all the time, the deeper, subcutaneous influences that really make those 'keepings' sound the way they do are quite concealed; you probably wouldn't find them. The real influences are more out of sight, at the level of what is really happening in the music. But at that age you're very porous, and I couldn't see any reason not to quote heavily when it came to me.

In a way that porousness was quite radical at that time.

I just remember it being the only possible way to go on at that point.

Was that partly a reaction against the pervasiveness of the exactly opposite view in compositional circles, the insistence on self-referential coherence that was the orthodoxy in some parts of British contemporary music?

I sensed that these elements might cause consternation here or there, yes. But I had no choice. I knew there were things in the music that would make people say, 'Oh, but you've borrowed that from x, y or z' – but in fact, they just came in by accident. Often a pattern I was already working with would suddenly throw up a suggestion so powerfully, like a face you see in wallpaper which once seen can never be unseen, that I would put it in – I didn't know you weren't supposed to. I mean, I probably did know, but I didn't understand why, so that for an artist is no reason.

These 'keepings' were also doorways into my own music. I'd find that whatever system I was using at that point would suddenly land me in a very definite key, like a lift door opening on an unexpected floor, and I would then use that as a door into a piece by somebody else. But that mostly happens in *Powder Her Face*, it doesn't happen in many other of my pieces. There was a feeling of Alice in Wonderland in that opera. I would write something, it would suggest a borrowing, I would push that borrowing into my own language and take it to an absurd point of distortion and from that, still other music would pop out. It is a dream logic, I suppose.

In a way, as you've written more music, you've started borrowing from yourself, because there are some tunes or harmonies that recur from piece to piece.

In some ways it's just like meeting the same person over and over again, but each time it means something else. For instance, for a while after I'd written my Piano Quintet, which ultimately had only one movement, I thought the piece was going to have a slow, serene second movement, so I started writing it straight away. It was a chimera, but for several months I felt that it was there, and that it was part of the Piano Quintet. And then I realised it was going to make the whole piece over an hour long, so I decided it was a Second Piano Quintet. But at the same time, an opera, *The Tempest*, was banging on the door. And so instead of being another quintet, that music ended up in the opera.

The material is closely related to what's now my Piano Quintet, but instead of being concerned with time and movement in a horizontal sense, this was concerned with vertical space. It's now Miranda's music, her first big aria in *The Tempest*, and also her duets with Ferdinand. So of course to the outside ear it couldn't be more different from the world of the Piano Quintet, but it's the same material and that's where it started. To me it's as if it's the same person, but in an entirely new light. And then I also put it in the second movement of my cello piece, *Lieux retrouvés*. That sort of transference of ideas is normal, essential even.

But although these pieces might use the same material, it feels like different music to you when it's in these various contexts?

To me, totally. If you think of the number of melodies there are in the world, they seem to be infinite. But the differences between them can be infinitesimal. All the tunes in *The Merry Widow* are the same four notes; *Parsifal* and 'Take a Pair of Sparkling Eyes' from *The Gondoliers* use the same notes. So the difference between them is not in the material. It's in the setting, in the lighting, the rhythm. Beethoven had a dry run for the 'Choral' Symphony in the *Choral Fantasy*. The first three notes of the tune for the chorus in that work are the same as the 'Ode to Joy', but then instead of going up, it goes down, and it starts on a weak beat as opposed to a strong beat. That's a really obvious case, because it's the same music. But one version makes a miniature fantasia, and the other makes the greatest symphonic movement.

When we think about classical composers, we tend not to have this issue. When we listen to a Mozart piano concerto, he's using the same figures, or versions of the same gestures, over and over again. But we don't have a problem with that, whereas in contemporary music, there's this idea, somehow, that each piece should be different, should be new. Why do we have an obsession with originality in new music?

Well, as I say, it doesn't bother me at all. How uninteresting to say, 'Never use the same notes again'. If you're a composer, you can't think like that. Of course artists are going to have obsessions that they return to. It's unheard of for that not to happen. And in my case it was a little bit like this: you know, you can throw a few chords down, and they'll be gone in three seconds; or you can look at the same chords under a microscope and trace a thread that holds them together, and that leads you in all sorts of new directions and it takes half an hour.

My piano concerto *In Seven Days* is a set of double variations, and one of the themes is a sequence of six chords. They're also in *The Tempest*. I always wanted to hear those chords played by four violins, one to a part, and one day I realised that I'd never done it in *The Tempest*. It was because the aria they're in, Ariel's song 'Five Fathoms Deep', needed to end with all the chords played by full orchestra, where she sings 'Sea nymphs hourly ring his knell', so I couldn't have my chords in just four parts. So then I took them out and made them the basis of *In Seven Days*, and I made them a theme of the piece. And now I've got them out of my system.

Do they mean the same thing in the opera and in In Seven Days?

No. They don't mean anything, on their own, they're just chords.

But aren't they different objects because of the different situations you press them into service for?

They're not a leitmotif.

I don't mean they connote cabbage or something.

Actually they do. *In Seven Days*, the third movement, that's exactly what it's about: the creation of vegetal life, on the Third Day. Look, if you put something under the microscope you see it has millions of implications. In the opera house, those chords are used at a moment where time is completely suspended, Ariel's hypnotising of Ferdinand. It is so strange, the image of ringing the funeral knell under the sea – we're in such a peculiar space. I thought, here we are somewhere we can't describe what's happening, Shakespeare has put a spell on us, and perhaps that's a way into some kind of pre-conscious space. Well, *In Seven Days* deals with the pre-conscious. It is the nearest I can imagine to writing a religious or devotional piece, almost. So that might be the connection.

Were you surprised with In Seven Days *to find yourself writing a religious piece?*

Well, of course not, it was my idea. Actually, I think that story of Genesis, which the whole piece describes, is as much scientific as it is religious. I was simply telling that story – the story of the material and also of 'material', all of it, in the world. It is a meeting-point between science and religion. I am sure when it was first written down, that Genesis myth, it was the last word in science. In fact it's almost exactly the order of events that we now believe, with one difference: the dry land and trees appear before the sun, moon and stars. But that is an improvement, aesthetically.

What about something more general? Let's take something like your fondness for harmonies based on stacked fifths, say, something you use in your Opus 1 right up to where you are now. If you looked at your use of that same idea in different contexts, what would it tell us?

If you're me, you would see that that's simply a result of a way of approaching firstly a fifth, and then how one fifth relates to another; and then rather than going in a circle, they would go in a sort of terraced shape. I mean, going further, that tells me a lot about one note. For me we're really talking about the fifth's inversion as an interval, the fourth – the same notes, say, F and C, but the other way round, with the F on top. The fourth is the most interesting interval, if you look at its history. Obviously it was considered a consonance in musical prehistory – pre-Monteverdi, let's say! At that time, before the seventeenth century, it was thought to be a stable interval. And over time something happened in people's ears, and suddenly the fourth was considered unstable. But for everyone from Pérotin to Palestrina, the fourth is a consonance.

And then it becomes a dissonance. It's mysterious, but it's something that happens in the cultural ear. In the textbooks, the fourth is supposed to resolve down to the third, so C and F should become C and E. But I absolutely don't want that. If you want to argue for the natural pre-eminence of 'tonality', you're supposed to believe that the fourth wants to resolve to a third. But it doesn't, to me. To me the stronger note is the top one. I hear a fourth as an inverted fifth; the top note is the bass. I don't know whether that is an evolution of the 'cultural ear' – perhaps it's just me, but I feel it as a fact.

However, if you progress that logically, and stack fourth upon fourth upon fourth, you wind up with total entropy, with all twelve notes of the chromatic scale as a sort of block. So to make the thing quiver and spring to life, I would want to move the upper one upwards by a semitone, so a fourth and one step above: C, F and then F sharp. In *Asyla* in fact it quivers by a quarter-tone either side and expands outwards in both directions. I start with the interval of a fourth in a lot of pieces, I've been drawn to that a lot. *Asyla*, *Living Toys*, *The Tempest*, *Powder Her Face* all start with a fourth of some kind.

Is that a conscious decision?

That question doesn't mean anything to me. You don't think 'I'll start with a fourth'. You must imagine that the fourth is an object, like a single note. It's an atom that is quivering, and it wants to split. And depending on the way that is done, something is generated. It can become a melody if played by a bass oboe with an accompaniment, as I do in the slow movement of *Asyla*, or if somebody sings it, as Prospero does in *The Tempest*. There are infinite ways it can go.

Is that your innate way of hearing or a choice you make?

I don't know. It's in my ear. Sometimes I think we are all just agents of a mass research, a mass evolution. I mean if Charles Babbage hadn't been born, I'm sure we'd still have computers.

When were you first aware of this way of hearing, this way of feeling?

Just now. I'm talking to you about it now. The thing is, it's just the noise I make. Look at the slow movement of the Franck Symphony, which is a very close model for the second movement of *Asyla*, now that I think about it, it's actually the same melodic structure. But it goes in a loop in my piece: that's what I've often done, taken something which has a latent pattern and absurdly extended it. But that Franck thing is actually a complete coincidence. I didn't notice until this morning that it was the same notes. I remember writing my melody down as a pattern, and noticing that it would fit only on the bass oboe. Then I thought of the texture with the cor anglais and pizzicato in the Franck, and turned it into the bass oboe with cowbells. Only this morning I realised by complete coincidence that those first three intervals are the same. Franck's melodies at once have this solid reality as melodies, like Tchaikovsky's, but they go even further: they have an instability, too. I find that symphony a very pregnant piece. It's wildly unfashionable now.

That phrase you often use has just come to my mind about the bass oboe melody in the slow movement of Asyla: *that it's a 'knight's move' away from the way that melodies might normally work . . .*

Indeed the shape itself is even like a knight's move.

Having written through some of the implications of this way of hearing intervals and melodies, you must hear differently now from how you did when you started composing. How has your way of hearing music changed?

I don't really think it matters, but you narrow down. When I was a teenager I used to listen voraciously. I used to record whole days of Radio 3 onto cassette – the more obscure the better. And I had a season ticket to the Proms and went to almost every concert. It was the best education for a composer. It might even be thinking about a piece: 'That was a total failure, so what did the composer do wrong?' Even more interesting is the ninety-nine per cent failure, because you then have to look at the one per cent that goes right. Like the Verdi opera I went to the other night: *Simon Boccanegra*. Artistically it's disastrous, but for some reason this music won't lie down and die. I admire how he can have such apparent lack of concern for the musical quality, but it still somehow has a kind of wriggling existence.

Do you feel the same about Donizetti or Bellini?

I love 'Casta diva' – that's the only Bellini I've ever heard.

What about Rossini?

I don't know the operas – although I saw the one about the nuns in bed [*Le Comte Ory*]. I love the overtures – what can one say? Much better than Verdi, who is very difficult for me. It's such poor material and it's often badly put together. I'm talking about the operas as whole works. *Simon Boccanegra* is like a bad joke: it's catastrophic from the point of view of plotting and artifice and pacing. Everything about it is wrong. It could hardly be worse. Yet it has this strangely powerful effect if it's done well. And I think the badness of the plot, the ludicrousness – it's not a period ludicrousness, by the way; it was ludicrous at the time as well – that very weakness liberates him, so that the music at times takes on a weird disembodied nobility. It's dis-embodied because the music is inessential to the drama. The drama's very ineptness seems to force him into being inspired.

Is there a damage-limitation side to writing opera?

To doing anything. The line is very thin. Verdi does have a raw native cunning, more in the better operas. And that means that often the poverty of the material is exposed, and I hate it all, and it is inessential. But I look at it in fascination, and I think: why is it that, despite everything, he can make a single moment that is so incredibly strong? Because those moments are stronger than they would be if someone had planned it properly. These things suddenly leap out, like a knife out of the canvas. For example, that phrase in *La traviata* that she repeats and repeats at exactly the same pitch while everyone else moves around her. You know everything about her at that moment.

How does he manage that?

Because he uses almost no brain. It's pure animal cunning. Isn't that clever? The thought that occurs to me is: 'How does he do this without any material? Do I ask the brain to do too much?' Well, no, maybe not. The rest of Verdi is too high a price to pay, for me. You look at something like the

Requiem, and it's kitsch. That's what he does when he's thinking about it. He makes something that is like a vulgar souvenir. It's truly vulgar, the Requiem, but brilliant, from beginning to end. It's very funny. For a Requiem.

What's the problem with kitsch?

This is a philosophical point – the difference between kitsch and cliché. In a funny way, if something is entirely cliché, it's not a problem. Plenty of masterpieces are just one cliché after another, Mozart for example, but that's quite natural, because if you think about it, two clichés that have never met each other before can beget the most original and profound effect. Kitsch is a cliché used in bad faith, where the person knows better, but still uses it, which causes embarrassment. It's an adult pretending to be a child. I wonder if Mozart is completely innocent, truthfully.

A composer like Niccolò Castiglioni, who died in 1996, is the opposite when he uses cliché: it's so obviously willed and controlled and planned, but childlike, so it's a total self-revelation. I looked at the score of a piece of his I heard recently, *Inverno in-ver*, and there was nothing there. But when you play it, it's extraordinary. It's eleven movements each describing frost in a different way. That's really putting something under the microscope. That's why Stravinsky liked him – there's nothing in it that's not cliché, and there's no shame, no guilt, and that makes it quite pure.

Is there a danger, though, that if you resist the bounds of 'good taste', whatever they are, things could become sentimental, if not actually kitsch?

You can only police yourself to a limited extent, in terms of taste. I try to be truthful. Maybe my music is to some people too emotional; to others, it's not emotional enough – you see, I can't think about it. Either direction is a result of not convincingly balancing the truth and the artifice – too dry or too mawkish – it's a question of artistic skill. That's where taste does come into play.

So you don't revise your pieces, even if you think there's something 'wrong' in there, something too 'mawkish'?

Well, if it's ruining the piece, you would – what I'm talking about is when the piece demands that, and that's what it had to be, even if in retrospect it seems beyond official 'good taste'. I've never revised to 'tone things down'. Only the opposite: when the effect wasn't strong enough, only ever to make the effect stronger.

Do you think there is a question of good and bad taste any more in terms of this chord or that chord?

Well, there was a time thirty years ago when a C major chord was a shocking thing in the context of modern music. People would jump out of their chairs. I saw literally that happen, with one of my teachers. It was F major, actually. But now it all depends, again, on context. *Tevot*, that orchestral piece of mine, opens with one sort of music high in the strings and woodwind. Then there is a C major chord low down, which is apparently unprepared. It doesn't feel like a C major chord from the 'Jupiter' Symphony, but it is C major. I thought, if we start there, what happens next? I remember thinking when this C major chord came into view, 'this means trouble', in terms of what its implications were going to be. A composer friend of mine heard it and used the word 'shocking' – he said I'd gone 'beyond taste'.

When I see you conduct your music – including Tevot *– your connection with the music you conduct is incredibly physically engaged; it seems to move you powerfully.*

That's lack of technique. I never had conducting lessons. And when you are conducting, you are describing the movement of the music in a way, and my music can move in quite extreme ways, so no wonder I sometimes almost fall over.

Are you aware you're moving your listeners, emotionally speaking?

I find the idea amazing. That to me is a miracle. I don't want to understand how it works. Speaking as the man who puts all the letters together to make the words – it's a miracle to find that anyone hears the whole sentence rather than analysing every letter as I do. I'm amazed that anyone can even follow it on that level, can actually read it with their ears; or be inside the building I have made, and be able to navigate its corridors, to feel where they are in the structure.

Amazed that they can read it without prior knowledge?

Well, that is certainly preferable. This is not about expertise or whatever. What on earth would be the point of writing only for experts? Anyone with ears can follow a piece of music if it's done right. Just as anyone with eyes can read a picture. I have no training in art, and so I feel very lucky if I look at a picture, for example, and suddenly have a sense of the idea in the painter's head and understand in a flash how we got from that to the thing on the wall. It's a moment when you are suddenly aware that you are standing in exactly the same place in relation to the canvas as the artist did when he or she painted it. And you suddenly fall through a hole into another place, actually. Not just a time. Another place, another world, but here.

That's what one wants when one listens to music, although I know it can't happen all the time.

That could be an illusion of yours, though: your idea of what the composer or painter thinks and feels might be the same as theirs, but it might be completely different.

It doesn't matter what the idea was – the important thing is that realisation that the thing is alive. It's not just an inert object in front of you, a famous painting or whatever. When you have that feeling, you're very lucky because you are suddenly inside a living organism. And it's a shock. And of course that's what I want to happen, that's what I'm doing when I'm writing something. I'm in the bowels of a real thing. When I'm listening to other people's music, that's my experience.

When did you last have that experience?

I always have it. But you know, it's usually occluded by a problem with performance or something distracting about the place or the people around me, so it can be elusive. But I always have it to a greater or lesser degree.

Then there's a professional question – of successfully building a vehicle, which will carry you from A to B or Z or wherever – from one place to another, back or not back. Some pieces are a return journey, other pieces are one-way. And at the end you are somewhere different from where you started. Or perhaps you are where you really were all along.

That's one's professional concern, and I'm obsessed with that, the idea of successfully making the piece convey. The piece has to be a vehicle that is capable of moving from one place to another. One doesn't want to be just watching a process happen. Because that's really not professional. That's academic. If you're going to do that, then be a professional academic, and do it properly.

What are the journeys that your music can take? Either they take you somewhere else and bring you home again, or they take you somewhere else and keep on going.

You've stumbled on the finale problem. They're a very big problem for everybody. Of course, if it's done right, the argument is not all over in the first movement, there is more to say and these further movements heighten and enrich things. And ideally, one is then in a position to have a satisfying finale. Beethoven's finales are often very unpredictable and inexplicable, because he is aware of the problem more acutely than anyone else and not one of his finales could be described as generic. With him it's often a release of tension. It's very rarely a sort of grand summing up: in the 'Eroica' it is, but that's a rather special case.

The Ninth?

What could be more unpredictable than that?

The Eighth too?

It's a total release – but the most amazing finale of that type is that of the 'Serioso' F minor string quartet, Op. 95. It's shocking. It's almost as though the piece can only achieve that sustained level of seriousness if he can suddenly let all the rabbits fly free, as he does, at the last minute. It's incredibly original and very difficult to bring off.

But then after Beethoven, through the nineteenth century, we get a big problem with finales, because no one was able to face the problem down and overcome it. Wagner avoided it, Brahms did it with a weary sense of duty. You usually feel his are there because we're supposed to have one. Tchaikovsky is always masterly. Look at the 'Pathétique': that Adagio is a very special kind of finale. It's the first one, perhaps, that admits it may all end in doom.

Do Mahler's finales offer solutions?

Mahler is interesting because he is one long series of problems, some brilliantly solved, some grappled with for

42

hours on end, some completely ignored. But he's always arguing with himself, all day and night long. He spends a lot of time arguing himself out of corners, especially in the finales. I find myself thinking: 'Why did you have to take the long way round? Why are you in that corner in the first place?' The Eighth Symphony is one long arguing yourself out of a corner.

He believed in it, though.

Well, I wonder. Of course, as a composer, you can talk yourself into these things. But then you look at the Ninth – and that's a person for whom all the certainties have completely fled. That's by far the most interesting of his symphonies to me in terms of material. Purely musically, the first movement is much simpler than the rest of his symphonies. It's even simpler than the First Symphony, in a way. But the implications are no longer worked out in the slightly mechanical way of the first two or three symphonies. They are fearlessly worked through.

Think about the melody at the beginning of the Ninth Symphony. It's just two notes, *mi–re*. You see the problem with that? It contains a fruitful paradox: it resolves onto a dissonance, which is an utterly Viennese paradox; it's in a lot of Strauss waltzes too. But it's obviously a total problem as the start of a symphony, because if the resolution is in itself a question, how do you ever get out of it? And vice versa. In that case he's arguing himself out of an extremely fertile musical problem, it's real musical territory, rather than the existential questions – 'Am I a hero or am I a waste of space?', all that – of his other symphonies.

Do you think he planned what would happen in the rest of the piece after he'd started the Ninth Symphony that way?

Oh no. If he'd planned, he'd never have started. That is why it's so moving when he does work through to a logical way of resolving that paradox. It's a very Viennese answer, a shrug which as if accidentally makes the problem disappear. It's very dextrous; the horns turn the *mi–re* on its head, *re–mi*, but it is inverted, so instead of ascending, it continues to descend, warmly, in thirds. It's also a good first movement from the point of view of the rest of the piece, because it leaves open a lot of difficult questions.

In your own music, where have you faced the issue of endings most keenly?

It's always there. One way I tried of ending things – I did this as early as in my Chamber Symphony – is suddenly to have an aerial view of the whole thing. *In Seven Days* also pulls the camera out at the end. *Tevot* does that, *Asyla* does that. In the Violin Concerto I worried very much about the end, which is different. When I was about ten, I used to play a game of guessing, with classical pieces, whether the end would be loud or soft. I thought those were the two kinds. I was usually wrong. I remember being very dismissive about *The Rite of Spring*, because I got it right.

Isn't the ending of the Violin Concerto more like a release than a cosmic zooming-out?

Well, there's an alternative version in my head, which is quiet, where the caravan moves on and fans out, endlessly.

That can often happen, an alternative, opposite ending, and it stays there like a ghost in your head for a while. For some reason that would have also been a true way to end the piece. I tried it, but it didn't stick. I'm glad it seems like a release – that's an odd one, because the first movement is already an aerial view.

You said that at the beginning of Mahler's Ninth Symphony, everything had already collapsed in terms of his vision of music, and possibly of the world too. So I wonder: where are we now? Are we in a time of stability or instability?

We're in a time of total freefall. Not even freefall – zero gravity.

In an end-of-all-things sort of sense?

No, why would that necessarily follow? What I mean is that we're aware that there is no floor and no ceiling, other than non-existence. So the only thing is to build something. You have to create where we are. There is no floor and no ceiling, and yet we are standing, so what on? What under? I love the lack of stability.

Even if the only choice is then to build false floors and ceilings out in the void?

Who says they are false? I think that there is no paradigm by which we can live. Paradigms by their very nature don't exist, they are not real, and things that don't exist are nothing. Ideologies, absolutes, are not things that one can really deal with. They might be theories, yes, but they're not there. They don't exist, they're dead. So that said, is one interested in them any more, or as a starting point; or does one say – much better – to hell with them?

It's a difficult situation, creatively, then: no absolutes, no paradigms, only floating . . .

Being alive is a difficult situation. But it's preferable to the alternative.

So you could say that you're constructing a set of floating viewpoints that give a perspective on that bigger instability, because without a point to observe it from, we can't actually see the big, unstable universe?

But that is what composers have always done, continuously. Think of Beethoven: there may have been paradigms in his mind, but he departs from them very quickly in practice. Of course, I would love to do something with such a perceptual solidity, or the diamond-like precision of Haydn or Nancarrow, because I am so aware of the chaos around us that I am attracted to those solid constructions. It was achieved by them, so one hopes that it can happen again.

3

material and form in the Piano Quintet – fetish notes –
Beethoven's 'Pastoral' Sonata as model – subjectivity and
objectivity – the consciousness of inert noises

What's the relationship between the material you use and the
form of your pieces? I'm thinking of a piece like your Piano
Quintet, which is cast in a sonata form – even with a repeated
exposition.

It's really the chicken and the egg. In that case, I just felt
that the way to work out this material would be a Piano
Quintet in a broadly sonata-form design, and that this
material would lend itself to a piece in that design. But you
have to realise that any sonata – well, any structure – isn't
an empty form that you just pour material into. It should
have been developed with the material in an organic way.
All that I wanted to do in my Piano Quintet was a sonata
form that gets from point to point, that conveys from the
beginning to the end.

In general, I don't believe that 'sonata form' is an abstract
thing that existed before the music. I'm quite certain of
that. At the same time, musical material that has its
own sap, and wants to run in a certain direction, can
also be a trap. It has to be got out of. You can hear that
happening at the very start of the Piano Quintet, in the first
violin solo. In the first three bars, it has already gone two
steps down a corridor and found a door, which won't open,

and then come back and retraced its steps, and returned to where it started. So it starts again, but goes only one step. The whole solo looks for a door that will open out of the material.

Then the piano comes in. And this is where my sense that when things are done twice they are at a different level comes in. It's rather like excavating a city, you find things underneath. That's why when the piano comes in with similar material to the violin, it's in B major rather than the violin's C. And it couldn't be in C; if it was in C, the piano entry would have a kind of classical confirmation to it, which is not really available after that opening, because everything in this piece tends to slip down, including the speed things are played at, which is never constant, always one level faster or slower than the phrase before.

The obstacle in the opening solo, the locked door, is an F. Now, this note has an important function in the whole piece. It's something in the way I hear all music, actually, this idea of there being a single note – a particular pitch on a particular instrument – that has a crucial function across whole structures. It's an analytical thing that I don't find reflected in written analysis enough, and it's something that I really feel is important. It's the idea of a fetish note in a piece: that certain specific pitches become fetish objects, which are returned to and rubbed by the composer all the time. It doesn't matter what key we're in, or what's happening around it in terms of the context of the music – that note on that instrument. You see it everywhere: in Beethoven or Mozart, Haydn or Chopin: there will be a note that will be a fulcral point for whole pieces. And often it won't be the tonic. Often it will be a note that has become an obsession, around which the whole piece hinges. There are so many Chopin Nocturnes that hinge on things like this. These fetish notes will often become an enharmonic point in the piece, a place where one kind of harmony can transform through a sleight of hand into another sort of harmonic area. But in order to do that, the note has to mean both things, to work in both harmonic worlds. To really understand the work properly, to unlock it – this is a key to something when you're performing – you have to hear those different meanings of that single note, and then you must play it differently every time. Whole symphonies are built around this: it's the grit in the oyster.

So in a way that is a fetish note – E sharp, F – in the Piano Quintet, and in fact it is a very specific note on the violin, one of the roughest notes, the first note played on the top string, with the first finger. It has an artless, primal quality, and of course one is very aware of it not just as a note on a page, but as a physical stopping of the open string by the left index finger. So in this movement it is like the grit in the oyster.

Think of it this way: when a child is learning about its environment, there will be some things they don't notice, and other things they will turn to again and again. It could just be an apparently random object; and that's how we sort of build our personalities, in a way: you build them around random things you touch repeatedly in a certain way, and your relationship with them will form around them.

Shortly before the end of the exposition of the Piano Quintet, there's a really striking moment, a place I've always found incredibly affecting. It's like an A major island of stability, something you can't mistake when you hear the piece, and it's all the more affecting, moving, because it comes in the context of all that slipping and continual transformation in the rest of the music.

Well, it's a version of the second subject that becomes a third subject. I'd always been fascinated by the idea of the third subject – if the first subject is a proposal, and the second a consequent counter-proposal, male and female or whatever you will, then the third subject becomes a mediating alternative of some kind. I was looking at a particular model of sonata form at the time, the first movement of Beethoven's 'Pastoral' Sonata, which was a piece I was obsessed with. I liked that model because it seemed to be a piece where the articulation of the drama was not very obvious, there wasn't an obvious opposition between first and second subjects, and the whole movement feels like one long organic process. I like it so much because it begins with a great instability. So in fact this music in my Quintet is quite close to the second subject of that sonata.

The piece also has the single most dissonant passage I can think of in any music you've written: the climax of the development, the central section.

I wrote a whole version of this before I revised it later. I knew what the music should be doing at this point, but I didn't know how to write it. I simply wrote the noise I wanted it to make: I did a caricature of it. That's a great temptation a lot of the time. I haven't often yielded to it, but I did do a caricature of it that time, and I knew, when we actually played it a year later, the Arditti Quartet and I, that it betrayed the piece. I knew I had to compose it in a different way to be true to the music, but that required another way of thinking. In order to write what became the final version of this section, I had to think very objectively. This is the most fraught section of the piece – and perhaps the most emotionally extreme – but I had to think completely objectively about it. If I thought about it in a subjective way, it came out like a kind of cartoon.

I felt that it had not come out right, it was a parody of what I wanted, because I had really cheated the material, and I couldn't do that in this structure. It was actually because I was composing in the wrong place. I was somewhere in America, Vermont, writing the piece in a room surrounded by trees. And the trees were a nightmare; all those organic things, they completely confused me. There was so much going on outside the window with all these leaves and branches, as far as the eye could see. I was not inspired; I was whatever the opposite of 'inspired' is. It just made so much 'musical' noise in the air that my own material and what it had to do became completely crowded out; it was all just smothered by leaves. And all I wrote there was this one section of the development.

And a year later we played it for the first time and I knew immediately I had to throw it away. Although actually one trace of it survives in the Quintet – in the region just before, where the quartet plays quavers on a repeated chord. And I'm quite happy to leave that part in, because it's a fore-shadowing of something that never actually happened. A ghost of a red herring. I think you find those in great music, in Beethoven, actually. The door we never opened.

Part of the problem with that section was trying to nego-tiate poles of subjectivity and objectivity – paradoxically, to achieve the 'subjective' emotional and expressive effect you wanted the music to have, you had to think, you had to compose, as objectively as possible.

But I don't really believe we have in the blue corner, subjective, and the red corner, objective. There's a certain kind of 'subjectivity' that is completely unhelpful – because it means not being at one with the material. If you say 'I want this' but the material wants something else, then you're not at one with the material. You have to try to be at one with it. So whether that's being objective or subjective is irrelevant. It's really one and the same, if it's working. I think if one's thinking inside the mind of your material, which you want to be anyway, that's what I mean when I say these chords have this kind of will, that becomes my will, too.

When you're making a work – any artist will have a little bit of this – you're trying to deal with the problem of being and consciousness in some way, really. And in the musical work particularly, you can end up with something that deals with that in a way that you couldn't through just speaking about it. So obviously the whole process is subjective, because all you have to work with is your mind and body. But on the other hand, it can't just be about the nervous system of the composer. That, in a way, doesn't get us very far. I have that problem with a lot of Shostakovich's music, for example.

When you are not aware of it, which I like, it's both subjective and objective at the same time. For example, Beethoven's most abstract works are also the most neurotic. Take the *Missa solemnis*, which is fantastically neurotic at all points. He has an obsessive intensity about his relationship with text at some points in that piece, and in other places, he is obviously totally impatient with it, like in the 'Resurrexit', which is just one line. It's a very irascible, impatient work. But at the same time, it's one of his most intensely wrought works, and what is always called abstract, with all those fugues. But they are fugues that come, as he said, directly from the heart.

So it does have oneness with its material?

Overwhelmingly. You can hear his mind through the operation of the material very powerfully. And he allows the power of the material its full rein, which involves at once total absorption in the self and a complete denial of what the self might want.

It seems to me you try to compose in a similar way.

Well, wouldn't we all? That's good – I don't know. I do have a faith in these things that in theory are just inert noises, that somewhere between my mind and these noises that are happening there is a connection. More than that – there's actually a consciousness. I can't explain to you why I know that to be the case. I'm not sure where I begin and it ends, actually.

*the subjects of pieces, and the world leaking in – hermetic
rooms and open doors in* Powder Her Face *and* The
Tempest *– the gratuitousness of art – performing and place
– institutions and practicalities –* Living Toys *and made-up
truths*

*Is there something in common about any story, any drama,
from* The Tempest *to Buñuel's film* The Exterminating
Angel, *that makes you think: this is a suitable subject for an
opera?*

Well, it's the question I ask with any opera: why would
these people not just leave the stage? Why are they stuck
here, singing, and why are we listening? I realise it's a
subject that preoccupied me quite early on. In a certain
way, that's what the subject of *Asyla* is, or *Traced Overhead*,
or that student piece *Catch*. What started me composing
was worrying why we build these things, why composers
or writers make a piece of music or a novel. 'Why' and
'how' are the same thing, here. At one point I thought it is
purely the creation of an alternative reality that one can
escape into. But now I think what happens is that you try to
create a simulacrum of the real world, a reflection. The
piece is a way of trying to make the real world real again, in
a sense. The earlier idea is a difficult position to maintain
through a lifetime, that composition is essentially an ideal
form of escape, because then you're thrown back at the end

of the piece into real life, to what's happened in the real world since the piece started. And so the escape has failed. Basically, I don't any longer think it's particularly fruitful to see art purely as an escape. Reality is always going to leak into the work to some extent. The question is how much you allow that leaking to take place.

I think this leaky relationship with the real world explains why, the moment a note is written down, for me, it immediately starts to move, it starts to slide down the page or up the page or move around. The extent to which you bully it and push it towards stability – that's what creates the energy in the piece and defines its position relative to reality. So, in terms of an opera, at the beginning of an opera: where are we? One of my favourite openings is Janáček's *The Cunning Little Vixen*, an opera largely about animals. The opening always makes me think of being in the garden as a child, and you pick up a stone and there are woodlice underneath it, and you are suddenly aware that there's a parallel world down there. That is a particular perspective in that opera. All operas have a different per-spective. *Vixen* has the beautiful quality of enlarging small things to a human scale – foxes and chickens and frogs – whereas if you compare that to Wagner, he's perhaps trying to do that to humans, blowing us up into mythological figures and gods and what-have-you. But you end up very quickly with a kind of absurd situation where Wagner is pretending that that kind of heroic thinking exists in reality, but this is false. The thing I quite like about *Götterdämmerung* is that it begins to collapse quite quickly. It ends with a sort of shrug, as reality begins to leak in; the reality of Wagner's pretence, and its lack of relationship with the world outside.

Because it's collapsing under the weight of its own delusions, its pretensions to the heroic and the mythic?

It simply becomes impossible, an impossible project. I wish it would become impossible much earlier on. By the end of *Götterdämmerung* the narcotic effects through which he tries to evoke that world have long since worn off, on me. Particularly in opera, you have to deal with the creation of atmosphere, emotional atmosphere. One can try to hold one's nose and say no, I'm above that, but in fact it is essential. But to me, this atmosphere shouldn't be something separate from everything else, extraneous to the notes. That would be merely decorative. And yet it needs to have a magical effect.

The material that you're using, the notes, is a collection of physical entities, of elements with distinct chemical properties. You're like a chemist, dealing with atoms and molecules; or the intervals might be particular kinds of drug, each with a different pharmaceutical property, used to various effect. Wagner is mixing huge complex potions: if they had scientific names, they would have sixteen syllables. But that to me is less interesting than someone who separates the elements so that you can see them all in their separate jars. I think that the fetish of giving the impression of development between these things – which is in some ways, you might say, a German compulsion – is to me a form of faking, an elaborate pretence. It can be a very powerful pretence and it does create new things; there is an alchemy there, in Wagner too. But I'm more interested in an art where you can see the different elements in a clear glass jar, or a Petri dish. In that case, the magic is even more powerful, more mysterious, because you can clearly see the elements that create this indefinable magic as separate entities. The tendency, the impulse, is to make something that conceals, something 'composed', but I actually work quite hard against that.

In all your work?

Yes, but particularly in opera: because if everything is connected, developed together – fused in a Wagnerian chemical concoction – then we don't have characters, really. All the characters are only facets of the same person, who is actually the creator of the opera. So in Wagner all the characters are aspects of Wagner, as it were, except for the ones who he thinks are ridiculous – and in my view even those. You're brought into his boudoir, into his private room, and there's this druggy, opiate smell, which you must submit to, and you become like him at the end, and that's boring. I don't find that it opens a door back into oneself, or back into reality in any way. It simply leads back into him, all the time. It's a snake eating its tail over and over again, and I find that uninteresting.

So the separation of elements, whether we're talking about instrumental music or opera, characters or themes, say, is also about separating them from yourself and your psychology or emotional life. In other words: giving them a life of their own.

If you separate the elements properly, you can catch a glimpse of chinks of light in the work, through which you can see through into some form of reality, an emotional reality that's not just a pathological response, nor an 'ouch' response, nor a mere reflex created by the chemicals in the music. It is an emotional response that is not pathological, where you can see the elements in the music separately and clearly and tell that there are two things happening that combine. Thus you get shafts of light, of reality, coming through into the opera. That to me is much more exciting.

So that means that the characters you create aren't 'your' characters at that point?

Well, they are, because the characters are defined precisely by musical relationships. I'm not talking about leitmotifs or something, which are obviously useful markers for someone in an opium haze, but I find them embarrassing. They're a kind of pantomime theatre to me. They're absurd, stuck on like Post-it notes to remind you what things are. But they aren't part of the organic life of the music, the veins and the tissues of the music.

You've used Wagner's materials in your own work, in Asyla *especially.*

That's true, all over *Asyla*, and the end of Act II of *Parsifal* at the end of *Ecstasio*. His influence is everywhere in music, his grubby fingerprints. Because the material is fascinating, but this is itself a problem, because one has to ask: 'Why are you not making pieces of music out of this material, instead of gargantuan soap operas?'

Well, because he wanted to change the world through myth, and he might say, 'Look, what you want is a less ambitious thing, because what you're trying to do is to create a little world

*in which there are chinks of light through to a bigger truth,'
whereas what he's trying to do is to create the whole world.
That's the difference!*

The problem again is the scale, because you should be able
to remake the whole world in two notes or four notes, like
Janáček, and indeed at his best Wagner got quite close to
that idea. Usually I hear an endless sequence of rich ideas,
like a series of brocades knitted together. The most
galvanising moment in *The Ring* is Hagen's call for the
vassals in Act II of *Götterdämmerung*: it is as though finally
Wagner stops trying to carpet over the fissure with his
interminable moth-eaten brocade, and we look down into
molten lava. It is a moment of pure destruction. You hear a
stable sound, a fifth, F sharp and D flat, but it is magnetised
always down to a tritone, F sharp and C; and there could be
no purer musical image for the end of stability, really. What
you have to see is that the 'Call to the Vassals' begins with
the crisis in the development of the 'Eroica'. It is exactly
that chord – in the Beethoven it is in first inversion, in
Wagner second, but it is the same, highly unusual chord at
the same pitch, and followed by the same, entirely
unorthodox chord as in the Beethoven, in a different
inversion and reduced to two pitches. Again, Wagner,
whether consciously or not, is clearly taking a crowbar into
the fissure that Beethoven found in 'Eroica' and prising it
open, for a moment. I hear it and feel this is what lies
beneath all of Wagner, but his nineteenth-century sensibility
forbade it; and indeed he retrenches straight away. But for
one chilling moment he is looking squarely at the crisis, at
the whites of its eyes. I find it impossible to hear, however,
without thinking of Nazis. When the vassals start appearing

59

and calling 'Hagen', I hear 'Hitler'. Wagner's immediate response to that inspiration of terror is brute stupidity. Everywhere else, apart from that one moment where he briefly looks right into the abyss over which he is laying his endless brocades, I hear his need to close the doors that he'd opened, and I find that embarrassing. I think it would be much more interesting just to go through a door and open more doors and find another door. As, in fact, to take someone from the same period, Liszt had done, or Berlioz. You never really know where you are going in Berlioz and to me that's much more real – the notes have a life of their own. I trust him more. I feel with Wagner something is being slipped into my drink.

For all your talk about 'opening doors', the subjects that you've set and the subjects you are setting concern situations that are hermetic, in a way: Prospero's island, the Duchess of Argyll's hotel room in Powder Her Face, *the inescapable room in the forthcoming* The Exterminating Angel.

Yes, but I think the thing is that there's a strong vacuum in those situations in my two operas, so that you're very aware of the pull of what's not there, what's outside the characters and the situation. *Powder Her Face*, for example, is about someone who's become a recluse, because her life has closed one door after another and the Duchess has trapped herself in every department, so she retreats into a world of perfume and fantasy and memory. The instability in that piece comes from the gap between what she wants to remember and what actually happened, because she sees it all as this glorious pageant, but that's not true. Her structure of denial, the lie that she has constructed, begins to fall apart during the course of the evening. The opera is a cumbersome way of conveying that, but the extravagance is the point. I think at that time I was fascinated by the gratuitousness of music. That was something I felt quite early: that art is gratuitous, we don't need to have it, practically, on one level. But then you think: 'What do we need to have? Is there really anything there?' So then, I think, well, art probably is the only thing we actually need to have, the only necessary thing, because it is the only route to the truth. Yet it is also gratuitous.

In that sense it's like scent, like somebody's perfume, as in the libretto at the beginning of the opera. This is why it started with a parody: we don't start with the woman on stage grandstanding about her life, we start with somebody taking the mickey out of her instead. This was a pre-emptive acknowledgement on our part that the whole idea is absurd, of walking in off the street and watching this woman go on about her perfume. But then I was hoping there would be a sense that one was fleetingly returning her glory to her life, just through the extravagance of the music in some places, through harmony itself. Then that is stripped away. In fact it was suggested to me by someone moralistic that I should have ended it with a sort of Triumph of her, because it would be more feminist. There's Anouilh's play on Joan of Arc, where instead of the burning at the stake, he ends it with a tableau of Joan as a triumphant historical figure from a picture book. But that's a banal way to deal with the story. It would be untrue and therefore to me uninteresting. And in any case that lighter finale wasn't available to me with the material that I had in *Powder Her Face*. It had to be a black full stop, that ending. It's as if every bit of the scenery on stage is folded up and packed away, and at the end the hotel room is empty. You know how there is nothing more final than a room that someone's lived in after people have been in and cleared everything out: it's an image of death. There are a lot of false bottoms in the harmony and I go through them all in the last pages: that was the only way I could finish it. Once all of those are closed, there's a kind of further harmonic door that's closed, of the whole opera, and it's a kind of *ad absurdum* ending of the piece.

What about The Tempest *and the hermetic space that opera inhabits – and the vacuum it leaves outside?*

With *The Tempest*, you have all these characters who are trying to get off the island – the only one who isn't is Caliban, who wants it all to himself, and at the end that's what happens. But offstage, there is Italy – rather like in *The Trojans*, you're never actually in Italy, but they sing about it all the time. In fact I quoted from *The Trojans*, where they sing 'We're going back to Italy', it's the same rhythm as 'Italie' in Berlioz's 'Royal Hunt and Storm'. So they're going home. You say it's hermetic: Prospero's relationship with the island is a metaphor for somebody who is cut off from his own life, cannot assume his role. First he was usurped from Milan; but the island isn't his either. The island is basically a kind of depression, and he has to make everybody else suffer it in order to dig his way out, because he has to prove to himself the redundancy of his power.

The redundancy of power – another connection with Powder Her Face, *with a cardboard Duke and a Duchess who is told that she is 'unfit to hold an ancient and honourable title'. And in* Powder Her Face, *your attraction to the subject was also the opportunity it offered to show the evanescence of worldly extravagance, opulence, luxury, and the morbidity of pleasure, of excess. This is very close to the 'vanitas' side of* The Tempest.

Yes, well, there is an aspect of the music that takes an un-English pleasure in the decorative. But that pleasure is really a cloud suspended above the earth, the way that music can seem to lift you off the earth. It is a form of rococo. The point is that it is not related to a moral code or a moral life of any kind. The music has its own morals.

You see, I'm not a composer who could write a piece that is nothing but physical pleasure, or indeed religious ecstasy – given that another function of pleasure in music can be to put the listener into a kind of religious trance. I'm suspicious of that: I'm too obsessed with consequences to be able to offer pleasure without consequence. In any kind of pleasurable experience, I'm always aware that I can see the ground rushing towards me. The question is whether you end the piece before you hit the ground.

Isn't part of the pleasure knowing that there's a dark side to these things?

Yes, that may add a poignancy. I'm not talking about payment, about redeeming one's pleasure with suffering or any such nonsense; I'm talking about the fact of, for example, the hangover. That's a physiological fact. But you are right, that consciousness of what you call 'the dark side' is something I identify in a lot of the light music that I was listening to.

Pop songs, folk music, you mean?

Anything: tango, *entre-deux-guerres* songs, Viennese light music, flamenco, popular song, whether it's an ancient song, a Middle Eastern melody, a Jewish song or other kind of folk song, or a pop song even. The texture of enjoyment of those things comes from the sense that you are one step ahead of a great black beast.

Because they represent a pure pleasure, for which there must, ultimately, be a consequence.

Of course, all these forms of music, at their best, are quite as emotionally sophisticated as any more formal music: they deal with extremely serious themes, loss and grief or religious feeling or whatever. I'm only really able to experience the pleasure when there is an awareness of that. I am rather morbid, and the only way to make that creative is to relish it. Then you are free to make decisions in the music that are the result not simply of a depressive impasse, but of recognising the twin natural impulses: towards pleasure and, at the same time, towards oblivion, even annihilation.

Would you say that you've always associated pleasure – the pleasure of a painting, the pleasure of food, maybe – with the same feeling?

Yes, it is much more intense when you're aware of its evanescence.

*The way you put it, it makes it sound as if it's a way of enhancing
the poignancy, in an aesthetic sense. But is it in fact something
you were never really conscious of – more your habitual way of
dealing with the world?*

How else could one deal with it? Perhaps one should trace
this. For some reason I started reading positivist philosophers when I was about fourteen. I can't remember why.
Around the same time I was being introduced to
Schenkerian analysis at the Guildhall School of Music and
Drama, and I suppose you might say it was a time when
that part of my brain, such as it is, was beginning to
function. To try to put the logical positivist idea very simply
– I believe it starts from Wittgenstein: there are only two
types of statement, types of sentence that you can say, apart
from ordering or questioning. Those two types are an
observation based on reality, or a tautology. There's nothing
else. And that made me think: 'What does that leave us?' If
that's true, there are no relationships, there's nothing.
Everything is simply dead, you put something down on
paper and it's dead. There's no echo to anything. There's
just a kind of matt surface that soaks everything up. This
thought put me into a form of intoxication of despair at
that point, and in order to escape that I started to think, 'I
have to make gratuitous things which stand outside this,
which the philosophers can't explain.' It's a privilege of
music that it can exist outside those statements. In fact I
was somehow very lucky at that point to have been endowed
in music, which is perhaps a world protected from that sort
of logical thinking, as the whole area of music is illogical, or
perhaps I should say supra-logical.

Was your encounter with Schenker important at that time?

I smelt a rat right away. I could tell there was something wrong. That rigid Schenkerian analysis which reduces a piece to three notes: why then have the piece? Where is the piece? It's dangerous nonsense. I know you think I'm deliberately missing the point of it, but I'm not. He seems to me one of those people who had a feeling that he ought to have a reason for existing and just attached himself to Beethoven or whoever.

Isn't it quite Wittgensteinian: that to you art, music, whatever, are basically illogical gratuities?

I think you have to know that it's gratuitous, to be thankful. I've no idea if I'll ever achieve this, but I imagine a miracle that one day might happen, that there will be a glint from this shiny unnecessary thing I've made, a ray that strikes reality in a light that makes visible the thing that supposedly can't be described: the present, perhaps. The gratuitousness of music is one's best chance of this.

That's an attitude to art, but surely that's an attitude to life as well?

I don't know. I live a relatively makeshift life. Sometimes I look at people who plan elaborate dinners or, you know, have a comfortable life with a wonderful wine cellar or whatever. I'd love to have those things, but I'm afraid I am only at home with a certain temporariness, an instability. I should live on a boat.

You are conscious of the transitoriness of home?

Every day, the evanescence of everything, including oneself. So I try to travel quite light. I usually fail. I mean, I'm not Jewish, but I carry a name of immemorial Jewish origin, and that awareness of the transitoriness of place – it may not be unrelated. I always had a slight sense that I wasn't completely rooted in one place. This may not be innate – I didn't know that there was any Jewish element to me until well into my twenties; it just wasn't a factor. And even when I did know, I had no idea what it might mean in terms of traditions, or patterns of thought. It was only later when I started to connect the argumentative way my mind works, with a certain scepticism, and the way I feel about certain questions of belonging – or not belonging – in an English place or even in a Christian place. Because looked at in that light, I'm 'three quarters Christian', but I was not schooled that way and I always felt detached from that side of things. I mean, I love some of the hymn tunes and Christmas – the pagan sense of the divinity of Nature overlaid with a decorative iconography is very British – but I can't follow the notion of buying universal redemption from sin with the coin of martyrdom. In fact the idea of sin, of a religious morality at all, is something I've only ever seen cause harm. Perhaps that is one reason I've never been able to accept the idea of Christ.

Even the gratuitousness of it you don't like, the aesthetic part of the story?

Now you're just being perverse. I don't want to get into religion. Although if you're going to be a composer, you'll be dealing with something which is not there, which doesn't exist. In fact, it's not there before you've written it, and it's not there after you've played it. It evaporates. Half the time you're also not even hearing the piece as it should be, depending on the performance.

Conversely, if you're recording a pop song, that will be the song, whatever happens to it afterwards, even if you have covers and you have people doing different versions of it, it's still a solid thing on that recording, as a moment in time which is perfected. Those exact four beats, the people in the room, that tempo, the sound of the drums, the sound of the guitars on that day: that's the song. But in classical music there is no such stability. No two performances of a piece are going to be the same. Alright, the score is there and it's fixed, but I know from experience it will never be the same twice, and not just because, in my case, much of my music is comparatively difficult to perform – despite working to make it simpler, it is difficult to play, more than I want it to be, but it just comes out that way. I try always to make it more reliable in the way I write it down but there's always a side of me which has a mistrust of reliability; is that a paradox? I don't know.

Why would you have a mistrust of reliability?

I aim to be truthful.

You're undermining the possibility for stability! Because it's already fundamentally unstable, you're making a piece even more so.

I'm allowing the instability. Now I'm increasingly finding

again the poignancy of pieces of music which pretend to be stable, the tragedy of that vain attempt: even a really bad piece, like *Carmina Burana* or something. But that's too bad to even talk about. The triumphs of Tchaikovsky, they have a very poignant fragility to them, the Apotheoses of the ballets or the finales of the Fourth or Fifth Symphonies ...

... which are banging out a kind of desired triumph ...

... and it is obvious this is just something that he wants to be true. But on the other hand, for that moment when it's happening, it is true, for a moment. There the escape is possible, if you like. I tried to do something like that with my Piano Quintet, which ends 'triumphantly', because it ends in a C major chord. But it's on the last semiquaver of the bar and there's a precipice of silence on the downbeat, which I hoped might make the frailty of the triumph more poignant.

Your relationship with performing is interesting: does all the travelling inevitably make you rootless in your existence? I know you're extremely rigorous in how you control your time, but nonetheless the demands you place on yourself as pianist and conductor, as interpreter of all of your major works, means you become globe-trottingly rootless. Is that also about ensuring a kind of performance practice will be created for your music, so that you can control what happens to it?

I learn a lot from doing it. But I don't expect to be filling concert halls and stadiums with my music; I'm not really interested in large masses. Indeed I actively don't want that, you can hear that in my music; I'm not thinking like that, and a consequence is that those who might listen to my music are not one undifferentiated group. I may not be able to see them in the dark, but I know that they are individuals. They're not part of a mass. I think my music ought to affect something in the individual; not something in the shared, lizard part of the brain, as perhaps some stadium music does.

Tell me about those different places you work in – where do you think your music fits, where does it dissonate? Where have you felt different sorts of reaction? I don't mean necessarily reception from individuals, or critical reception; I mean a feeling about your music that you've physically experienced in different places.

I don't notice, because the audience are individuals, not 'Berliners' or 'Brazilians' or 'schoolchildren' or any other mass that some journalist has invented. I don't write the blurb. Early on in your career, the adjectives you're going to get might be things like 'challenging', 'innovative' or whatever. Then it could be 'acclaimed', 'award-winning'. It's all nothing. Although I was advertised as an *enfant terrible* or something again the other day and I rang them and said, 'I'm forty. You'd better think of another phrase.' Another nonsense. I was relatively young when I started, but I didn't get anywhere near what I wanted to do until quite recently. Besides, how can one second-guess what any individual will think?

You write for pre-existing classical music establishments, in a way that a lot of composers don't: they write for ensembles of forty guitars, say, unusual ensembles, anything but those institutions. But you write for string quartets, orchestras.

I wouldn't read anything into that. I have written for plenty of unusual instruments. But unusual sounds are not by themselves enough, for me, as a starting point. To think, 'I'm going to have this weird ensemble and go from there' – that's dangerous, because the piece could become a hostage to that idea. The orchestra, as a basic palette, still has the most variety. Writing *Asyla*, a piece for symphony orchestra, I became aware during the composition that the piece needed to emerge from this sound of tuned cowbells and a piano tuned a quarter-tone flat . . .

. . . which are certainly not part of a standard orchestra, that's the point.

Quite, but to me, that's not the point. I don't approach it from that angle; I didn't think of those sounds as something outside the piece. In Bruckner, you start with a tremolo, which wasn't a standard way to start a symphony then. So that for me was the piano tuned a quarter-tone flat. I didn't put it in to be 'exotic'. It is part of the symphonic idea, the context. Also the cowbells enter the bloodstream of the music. They've been a symbol of 'elsewhere' in symphonic music. 'Elsewhere' is a most important word for me. It was André Breton who said, 'Life is elsewhere.' The cowbells in *Asyla* become a metaphor for Elsewhere, as in Mahler or Webern, although there the cowbells are not tuned.

Have you ever regretted not being more practical? After the premiere of Living Toys, *for example, where the reaction of the conductor, Oliver Knussen, was that you had to simplify the notation, you then published the score with the suggested beatings.*

He was quite right. I had many hundred bars with one beat to the bar, and everyone was getting lost, and every time I've been to a performance of that piece, the musicians get catastrophically lost. I have often regretted rash, impractical things, like an anxious father; but still I realise that to have been more cautious, or to change it, might have made it anodyne. Today, I might pragmatically do it in a slightly different way. That piece is slightly like a changeling, an alien child, to me, though I do recognise it as mine. It is written on the nerves and I don't normally like music that's written too much on the nerves.

Why?

Because the personality of the composer becomes more important than the personality of the piece. I'm too conscious of myself in *Living Toys*, and that's not interesting to me. It feels like somebody putting on a coat that's the wrong size.

A very beautiful coat, I've got to say, but just a bit wee for you?

Too big, too small, I don't know. I invented this story, which is in the score, and said it was 'from the Spanish': that was after I'd written the piece, and I felt I had to find a way of explaining it. Wrongly, of course. Music is its own excuse.

So there were no images in your mind when you were composing the piece?

Well – there were titles, names.

You had the names?

'Aurochs and Angels', the two first parts. That's from the last paragraph of *Lolita*, which is central from the point of view of what we're talking about in terms of the relation of art to life. In Nabokov there's always a real situation behind all these extravagantly beautiful images, which is often rather sad and pathetic. There is a passage in *King, Queen, Knave* where the hero breaks his glasses, and there's a description of Berlin seen through the broken glasses which makes it seem the most fabulous thing that could possibly have happened, this dazzling vision, when of course it was really a pain in the neck. I was twenty-one, so all these literary influences are very near the surface.

But the story you write in Living Toys *is in a way a kind of truth-telling, because it's about the experience of the piece as sound, transformed into metaphor.*

Seen generously, it was a truthful way of describing the piece. It was my version of Schenkerian analysis, to do it that way, as a fiction. In fact, the last part of the piece, the funeral part, I'd already written; it came from an exercise I wrote for a student course, which was the first time I had the experience of writing something and then, when it was played, finding it turned into something completely other. I wrote what was a combination of two things, and in practice, a third, quite unexpected thing happened, in the harmony, that I hadn't anticipated. Not just another chord: it created a new direction. That was the first of many times that's happened. That's one of the most exciting experiences you can have.

After you wrote Living Toys, *you started to put the metaphor into movement titles, in* Arcadiana, *for string quartet.*

I wanted to marshal the idea of a symphony as a sequence of narratives, to delineate seven specific topoi within each of the seven different movements, which in their relation to each other would outline an eighth, unheard idea.

They're images of Elsewhere in Arcadiana *too, I suppose.*

Elsewhere, or a here that has gone, or is going. I suppose the eighth idea would be where we really are.

5

*Stravinsky as terminus and inspiration – style-blindness and
real substance – Fragonard and Feldman – the historical and
musical moment, Beethoven's First Symphony and* Missa
solemnis *– Berlioz the curmudgeon, Berlioz the first
Modernist – the necessity of being improper*

*You perform more of Stravinsky's music than you do any other
composer.*

For a composer, Stravinsky is like a terminus that you have
to go through to get anywhere on the train. There's no way
to avoid him; and I'm fortunate in that I love everything he
did and find so much to learn from. I think you will get
further if you're learning from examples that you can't
replicate that easily, that run counter to your own nature. In
other words, the structures in his music tend to be hard-
edged, there isn't much transition; whereas looked at in one
way my music is naturally always transitioning, always
slipping, it's always volatile. But no composer has worked
through as many shifts of style as Stravinsky. So the value
of that, now, as an example, is immeasurable. And often
with influences, one is a face at the window, looking in
on something one wants. Following Stravinsky's principle
that 'A good composer doesn't borrow, he steals', I took
the melody from the sarabande in the final act of *The
Rake's Progress*.

75

Where is it?

It's at the moment at the end of the courtroom scene in *Powder Her Face*, the trial, Scene 6, when the Duchess leaves the courtroom and the crowd say, 'There she is, old trollop.' It's as if she becomes the bearded lady, Baba the Turk from *The Rake's Progress*, at that point. So this rather obvious parallel in the music emerged. It came out of what my music was already doing – it was like a skin on the milk that formed and I just didn't skim it off.

The odd thing is, in the Stravinsky, it's one of the many moments in that piece where you see an earlier perspective of his music coming in, as opposed to the new direction he was taking. A lot of his music, throughout his life, is saying goodbye to a former type of writing at the same time as welcoming a new one. All of it, maybe. In *The Rake's Progress*, it's almost as though the material has a tenderness, it's soft and malleable because it's preparing for a metamorphosis; it's the end of one thing, the disintegration of one way of thinking and the beginning of another one, which makes it softer, like a crab before its new shell hardens. When I used that music from *The Rake's Progress* I hadn't really looked at how it was constructed physically. I just knew the music and loved it. So the construction in my opera is my own. But that often happens. You love something for years and you don't really look at it scientifically. But an influence in some way creeps in under the skin.

You seem to be saying that it is the huge distance between your style and that of another composer whom you love, say Stravinsky, that creates a fruitful model. What exactly is the nature of that dissimilarity?

Well, part of the fascination for me of Stravinsky's writing is that it's almost as though his ink has a kind of built-in fixative. The moment the note hits the paper, bang, it sticks. Like a dart in a dartboard. And it's partly this physical sense of intervals and that famous description he had of them being like testicular eggs that weigh in a certain balance. Dalí-like. There's something that I do recognise there, talking of the two notes that make up an interval as having relative weights. That's territory that I'm finding increasingly useful, particularly in the music I've been doing last year, like *Polaris*, because I wanted to look at how you could perhaps hold something in suspension.

Stravinsky's solidity attracts you because it's something you feel you lack but would like to have?

That's normal. Look at Schubert writing all those fugues, which was not his forte, because he felt he needed better counterpoint. And after all perhaps it did benefit his songs. So with Stravinsky the lesson might be: how can you hold two notes in a fixed relation and still make a living structure? Because that is not something that comes naturally to me, I want to do it.

Is there not a fear of actually sounding like Stravinsky?

Oh, not in a million years, because what I'm talking about is compositional practice, something purely technical, not style. All non-composers hear style, surface, far too much. To me it is a mirage; I see through it, not necessarily in any more intelligent way, but just because I have eyes that are looking for the 'how' rather than the 'what', because I have to understand. It doesn't seem real to me, the style of a piece. It never has done. It always seems not only the least interesting thing, but simply so transparent to me that it is not there. I've always been bewildered by talk of style. If you admit something is a surface – then it's a surface. I mean: eighteenth-century 'style', romantic 'style', these words are literally superficial.

This realisation makes one vulnerable to charges of 'eclecticism'. I mean it may sound ridiculous to you to describe it as a crime, but you'd think it is in some places. Because I'm style-blind. Well, not blind, of course I can see what people think they mean. It's not like colour-blindness. I can see the difference between Italianate ornamentation and, I don't know, Germanic counterpoint. But I can also see that the reality of the music is behind that, it's not in these surfaces.

But that is odd to me, because I'm also fascinated by surface, the play of surfaces, in a way that's not to do with style. So I realise I can be quite vulnerable, particularly because I'm fascinated by location and topography – setting a piece in a location, even if it's an abstract piece, like Beethoven does. All of his work, say, a sonata movement – it has a topos. The topos might be a cantilena, or a recitative and aria, or it might be pastoral, or it might be a tempest scene, or it might be any number of things in one movement. It might just be a little scene with two people in a wooded glade. I think a lot of his pieces are that. It might be a dance with the faeries. He doesn't call it these things, but the point is the pieces have a location. The greatest symphonists have that, Haydn, Beethoven, Sibelius. It's a very honest praxis. And often the symphonic dialogue is a struggle between that topos, or genre, and some logic in the material. That goes through from Haydn, where for example a simple tune like that in the finale of the 'Joke' Quartet has to perform critical structural operations – like the final cadence – and the genius of it, so much more profound than a joke, is that it does so simply by returning to itself; through Beethoven, where it is an animating principle almost everywhere; to something like Sibelius's Fifth Symphony where the simplicity of the, as-it-were, dance tune, or folk tune, *kantele* tune or whatever it is, of the slow movement, is pulled out of shape in all directions by the magnetised rock of the clashing tonal material around it.

So then I have to look very hard at what it is in my music, what is the topos. And I believe that there's no separation between that and the material, the notes. It's simply: does one leave the surface on, or not, like the skin on milk. It's not exactly masks. It's transparent masks. Even nakedness, 'no style', is a form of clothing, of drag, in that sense. So we have to be honest about these things and not be ashamed to say, 'Oh this? I got it in the sixteenth century,' or whatever. Some people get horrified by this. But if the composer has properly heard beneath these surfaces, you are not really conscious of them: you just see the beauty of the form beneath, the truth of the emotion. Coming to write an opera that's set in whatever past century it's supposed to be, as in *The Tempest*, say, you're dealing with politicians in a lot of it, people very much attached to their era. I needed to find an archaistic style, which, at the same time, was not specifically archaic, didn't pin it to one particular period too much. But the important point was not the style, the skin; it was the emotion in the veins.

Now the point is, the same would be true in an opera set in London in 2011. This is a really tough subject. There is a drag available for that, which is the 'gritty urban today', whatever you want to call it, but if you really look at it, you'll find that is also cobbled together from patches of other things, old things. I think unless you're very sure of what you're doing, you're going to obscure what is actually happening underneath the surface by pretending that your surface is 'real'. Whereas what I hope to do is make what's underneath the surface clearer, by making it honestly unignorable that the surface is just that – transparent, evanescent – and moving through the available material in such a way that the real form becomes clearer. So that may actually involve some things from the dressing-up box. But if the underlying form is clear, it absolutely doesn't matter that 'Oh that's an old bit of whoever'.

So the eighteenth-century surface of some of the court music in The Tempest *is just that, a surface?*

It might be helpful to draw an analogy with painting. When people look at a rococo painting now, like a Fragonard of a park, they might just look for a second and think 'swirly', and that's that, it's the French eighteenth century and that's all there is to it. But that's not how it came into being. Whether the artist wanted to create a mood, or some kind of transported state of mind in the viewer, or an idealised physical space with deep volumes and perspectives, or all of the above, it's not necessarily given to us to know what he might have been intending, what the underlying form is that preceded the picture. But when I look at it I am conscious of impulses in it that reflect mine, and instantly the centuries between us are dissolved. I think that's why I love the rococo so much, because I feel aware of the in-joke, that it's about much more than swirls and putti.

This was a period of art that the Modernists rejected completely.

Quite wrongly. And even if you read somebody who should be more intelligent, like Morton Feldman, he thought Fragonard 'ridiculous'. For Modernism, any kind of art that was not stripped down to a Barnett Newman type of abstraction was ridiculously 'literary'. But you can't avoid meaning; and in any case, why should you want to? All he was really saying was, 'It's incredibly unfashionable, unlike me. I'm Morton Feldman, professional Modernist.' But he didn't even bother to say that, because at that time, in the Fifties or Sixties, it was so obvious to everybody that the French rococo was beyond the pale and could never be rehabilitated, that all you had to say was the name 'Fragonard', and everyone would laugh. But now I look at that and think, 'Who's laughing now, Morton Feldman?'

I just think that was a disgrace, that whole project. It was endemic at that time. You couldn't stand outside it without looking like a fool. It took someone acting the fool – Ligeti – to break out of it. What was wrong with that period was that it didn't see that that form of stripped-down Modernist aesthetic was just as much drag as was rococo; more so, in fact, because it was not honest about it. It didn't dare to acknowledge that 'Modern' was just another style. If you really wanted to play that game, then the only thing that mattered was the surface, and therefore you stripped it down. You were really completely missing the point about a frankly much greater period in art where there was a huge attention paid to surface. To me, the rococo has much more depth. The surface is not saying what it appears to be saying. It's saying many more things. There's a mystery there. I think that if you damn someone or something simply on grounds of style, you're exposing a total ignorance of what is really going on. You're showing a failure to understand how things are really done, what they mean, what they are at all.

So style is a red herring?

Well, in order to be understood, it has also to be seen through completely – like anything, actually.

It's not as simple as saying, 'There's a surface and behind it is an idea,' in terms of painting or music or anything else? The style is part of the idea?

Yes. In fact you need to recognise that the surface is almost like skin, real human skin, the epidermis, which is just a sequence of translucent layers. The top layer is translucent, but if you look at it on a person, you don't see it as translucent. You see it as opaque. But it isn't. Do you know what I mean? If we started unpeeling ourselves, each layer would be see-through, but we're not see-through when we're put together. That's what style is. That's all it is. What people lazily call style is only the top surface of the skin. But it's all – in something that's any good – *cellular material*. So that, in fact, there is no such thing as style. It is all idea. I hope we're all intelligent enough to realise I'm not saying, 'I'll just write in any old style I feel like.' I'm saying the opposite: it is not about style. Style is for critics. That's all. It doesn't exist. If a piece is all style, it isn't real. This is not to say,

'Write in any style you like, whatever it is.' I'm not really saying that at all. There's banality lurking in both directions.

Banality in the direction that seems to peel everything back, like the old-fashioned Modernism, and banality in the other direction which seeks to mimic a style, like the old-fashioned post-modernism? Both are obsessed with surface?

Either label is missing the point.

Did Stravinsky avoid this kind of kitsch, for you?

He walked such a beautiful middle way, between borrowed surfaces and live material. Sometimes he trespasses outrageously, in both directions. He's the great example of someone for whom the style of each piece is a transparent thing that reveals the energy beneath. He could be incredibly severe, unyieldingly naked, or should I say flayed, in his later works. And he could be extravagantly cheesy, particularly in the Twenties and Thirties, wildly, provocatively tasteless. *Oedipus Rex* is a hoot. Imagine doing an art deco oratorio based on the most grisly Greek tragedy, with all these circus tunes mixed with Italian opera mannerism. It shouldn't work. It should just be a joke, like a lot of Poulenc, whom I love, but though the *Gloria* is a wonderful thing, somehow it just isn't great. It's fabulous, but it's not great. But *Oedipus Rex* is great, to me. That is real power. But it's rather a shock when it turns out to have so much power at the end, because you suddenly realise after all the jokes that it's deadly serious.

And there's no contradiction there?

That's precisely the point.

What else have you seen in Stravinsky to follow as a model?

Oh, good heavens – well, composers are all dealing with the same problems over and over again, but when somebody has dealt successfully with so many of them, and over such a critical period, when almost everything else was falling apart for decades, it's inevitably going to have a great deal to say to us. And we've come nowhere near the end of what he has to say to us. We haven't got to the end of what Beethoven has to say to us, for similar reasons.

That raises the question of historicity, of what and how this music still means to us today, and what it meant in its own time – I mean how much it is moored to its own time, how much it transcends it through some alchemy of historical situation, place and idea. What's the relationship, in the music you most admire, between how we hear it now and the time and times in which it was written?

If you look at, for example, the opening of Beethoven's First Symphony, why would it not have been possible for Mozart to start a symphony like that? The chord itself, a simple dominant seventh, was, of course, entirely available to Mozart: he used it a million times, and indeed, so did everybody else for centuries before Beethoven. But it would not have been possible for Mozart to write that chord as the opening of a symphony. It was, what, ten years after Mozart's death?

Yes, it was published in 1801.

So he would have been forty-five. But even if he had lived to be seventy, eighty years old, I still don't think he could have done it. Somehow it represents a leap of imagination, a step through a door that was there in Mozart's time but to which the key had not been found. And of course, on one level, all it took was to write the thing down; but it's much more than that. You just couldn't see over that wall then. Ten years is no time at all. But just the idea of beginning with the tonic, but as a dominant seventh, would not have been possible for a man of Mozart's generation. It would have been too improper. It's so extraordinary, really, because it immediately says, 'Yes, the tonic is unstable,' and yet it also ultimately makes the home key stronger. So it is a paradox. In one moment, that chord is the birth of a new world. I don't think Mozart would have been able to begin a symphony with a pizzicato either. Somebody will prove me wrong. The point is that all of those elements were available to him. What was not available was the idea. The metaphor was not available because it could not have been thought yet. The material was available, but not the idea. And it's nothing to do with the French revolution or any of that historical tangentiality. Was pizzicato illegal in pre-revolutionary Europe? No.

Or take the opening of Beethoven's *Missa solemnis*, when the orchestra enters on a weak beat and the timpani and the trumpet play the downbeat. And of course, in Handel's day, or Bach's, it would simply have sounded as if half the orchestra had come in early. It would not have meant anything beyond that an error had occurred – maybe someone at the back of the orchestra was drunk. But it's actually just a D major chord. So the notes were all there, but the idea of half the orchestra entering early wasn't, before Beethoven. Obviously it's a very specific thing that is happening there. It's a kind of breathing in, in which you've already breathed in the whole piece, as that upbeat. And even at that stage in his life, I feel that that was a very painful decision, a very painful opening to come up with. You can feel the struggle in it. It may not have seemed sublimely inspired at the time, but that opening would not have been possible fifty, even five years before because it would have sounded ridiculous. It would have sounded like a mistake, and yet to us it does not sound ridiculous. Can you imagine the *Missa solemnis* opening with everybody together on the bar line? It wouldn't be the *Missa solemnis*. It would be banal. The difference in some ways is tiny but, of course, it's everything.

So it is important to belong to your time, in order to be ahead of it. This is frustrating, because it might take you, I don't know, three months to write ten or fifteen seconds of music. So that also means that your timescale is completely at odds with everyday life. However, I think, increasingly, one has to understand that if you look back through time, artists have to be somehow of their time, or ahead of it, but not completely opposed to it. I don't think that's possible. I think that's a very difficult and almost certainly unhelpful position for an artist to take. As much as writing only for one's time. That's also unhelpful. I think this is about relevance: I wouldn't chase after it, as it is always moving; but it's probably not wise deliberately to avoid it. However, if you chase it to the exclusion of your own wishes, you won't get far.

The point, then, is that those leaps of idea could not have been made ten years earlier. Are things available to you in 2012, similar doors, that weren't available to you in, say, 2002?

I don't know. No one knows. That's the point; they might be there but that wouldn't mean one could find the door. Let's look at it this way. We hear Beethoven and it speaks to us as something that is alive. But if he were to hear our music of today, he would think it was a joke. One suspects. We can't know. But that would be very likely. Even someone like, let's say, Berlioz – in whom one can actually watch a change happening in his lifetime. He starts off being a progressive, who takes the most enormous imaginative step in music – not in the profound ideistic way of Beethoven's step, but in terms of material and the way of putting things together – in the *Symphonie fantastique*. A giant leap. But then, at the end of his life, you could mistake him for a curmudgeon, for an old fart, really. Although it's actually, as so often with curmudgeonly old farts, a form of youthful mockery and satire that's turned in on itself. That's very common.

So his last work, Béatrice et Bénédict, *is curmudgeonly?*

Béatrice et Bénédict has perhaps the greatest ten or fifteen minutes Berlioz ever wrote: the duet for the two women, so sublime. It is the culmination, the distillation of that seam of amatory nocturnes in Berlioz that runs from *Les Nuits d'été* through Didon and Énée's duet in *Les Troyens*, although in this case all the more moving that the duo are friends rather than lovers. But he had this quixotic obsession – even in *La Damnation de Faust*, which is much earlier

– with bad academic fugal choral writing. And unfortunately, paradoxically, that meant that he wrote a lot of them, but they were always satirical. But it's not a joke that really works now. Frankly, it's a bore. And there are yards of that in *Béatrice et Bénédict*, I'm afraid, too much. *Les Troyens*, however, is another of those pieces that, like *The Rake's Progress*, has so much to tell us because it is on a cusp in some ways.

A stylistic cusp?

Yes. I wish you wouldn't use the word 'stylistically' though. It doesn't mean anything. It's really a cusp of method. Anyway, this has damaged *Les Troyens'* career as an opera because, again, most people just hear what they think of as the 'style', which they see as a recidivist neo-classic style, which is, of course, almost always very unfashionable. *The Rake's Progress* encountered similar problems at first but ultimately suffered less because it had a lot less competition from its contemporaries. But in *Symphonie fantastique* Berlioz had made the greatest revolutionary step in music, a greater step from what immediately preceded it than, say, *The Rite of Spring*, which is actually close to Rimsky-Korsakov and Tchaikovsky. Compare the 'Scène aux champs' to the 'Scene by the Brook' in the 'Pastoral' Symphony: it is the same idea, and you can even hear the same bird, the quail, as in the Beethoven; but Berlioz is describing someone who has taken opium, perhaps the night before, and is alone in the countryside, cold – you can feel the cold in the textures – and paranoid. The countryside is described from a paranoiac perspective. In that single step away from Beethoven, Berlioz has brought us into the

Modern world of relativity and uncertainty. That step into the Modern is thought to be the twentieth-century step, but it is actually a nineteenth-century step, taken by Berlioz first of all.

So anyway, imagine Berlioz materialised in twenty-first-century London and you played him something from the last twenty years. I suspect he would simply be bewildered. He'd understand what the notes were and perhaps what was happening, but he would think, 'This is impossible.' He would simply find it *bad*. So I can't go through the doors that are going to be available for somebody in a hundred years' time. It would be meaningless to do so. In a way, it's the extent to which we can allow ourselves to be *bad* in our lifetimes. Breaking new ground is to do with doing things that were previously thought to be, in a way, too rough or too crude or just an awful noise or just plain *bad*. That's quite commonly the case.

Things that break the rules, then?

Yes, but I'm not talking about rules in terms of what might be in an academic rulebook. I'm talking about the rules of sensibility.

So are there things you're consciously trying to break?

No, it's not done like that. Not at all, that's boring. That I think was maybe the way things looked in the twentieth century. At least to teachers and critics, who can only see these things after the event. It's simply a natural moving forward; you are moving at the pace of time. Much of the 'Scène aux champs' is very close to Beethoven, in terms of the actual notes. It is the sensibility that has completely changed, so the language is changing from within. I mean, there are those people who are ahead of their time and go too fast, people who are doomed to be 'rediscovered' over and over again by someone with nothing better to do, Havergal Brian or Rued Langgaard or whoever. They aren't really very good. Those marginal, 'ahead-of-their-time' people can be interesting in some ways, but they didn't really understand what they were doing. But then you have Mahler, Janáček, even Berlioz himself, who were at one time considered in that way. Nancarrow too.

There can be a blurring. Ives was regarded as a composer like that for a long time, and actually I think *was* a little bit, but in fact, of course, he is a great artist who is going about it in the right way, although he flirts with amateurism. He didn't care about that, because he was in a country where those distinctions didn't matter. But yes, if you go too fast, you're going to risk looking unprofessional. You will have to be prepared for people to say, 'You don't know what you're doing. You're just throwing notes around.' It's the same with instrumental writing. 'That note isn't on the instrument,' musicians say to you – when actually it is. With a great composer like Nancarrow, who is ahead of his time and worked virtually undiscovered for decades, it is more as though time is behind him! You will be thought improper. I think one has to run the risk of being thought improper by all sides.

Do you have improper moments?

I hope so.

What are the moments when you think you might have been seen to be improper?

I don't know. You can just feel it while you put the note down.

There must be something you're thinking of.

Things you do can cause bafflement and I don't know why. I'm not interested in other people's private lives.

What is potentially improper, then?

I'm afraid anything that's likely to go anywhere is going to give you that feeling, that surely it isn't quite proper.

And what defines the 'proper'?

Something that goes over familiar ground in a reassuring way, obeying the approved pieties of the day. That's a waste of time.

6

*not listening, but conducting – writing for individuals, not
'people' – playing and conducting other composers' music –*
Arcadiana *and outside – the variability of live concerts –
virtuosity and the defiance of fate – Beethoven's coffee
beans – playing and recording a cancan –
new worlds*

*What's the difference between listening to your music
and conducting or performing it; say, between sitting in the
dark watching* The Tempest *and being up there conducting
it?*

I don't like to listen to my own music at all, after it's written.
All I hear is what's wrong with it.

Yet you're totally happy to conduct it?

Oh yes, but that's helping people. I'm not actually making
any noise. It's only people who are playing it who are
making noises.

*But surely you're listening to it as well when you're conduct-
ing it!*

But only to make sure it's together. You have a point,
because I'm going through it in time when I'm conducting
it. But when I then sit back and listen to my music without
conducting, I'm a different person. I'm engaging critically

in my music, and that's uncomfortable, when the experience of making the thing was nothing but critical the whole time I was writing it. And I'm afraid when I then hear it, all I do from the moment it starts is hear all the things that are wrong with it and that are missing and are just not right. It's like seeing a video of oneself acting or something. It's excruciating.

So actually conducting your own music is, in a way, an escape from having to deal critically with it.

Well, I'm not self-conscious when I'm conducting, which means I am freer to enjoy it. I'm doing a job, after all.

So you do enjoy it?

Of course, but I enjoy it more now that I have a little more technique. I didn't have technique for a long time. I never had conducting training, so as a result I used to get exhausted, much more tired than a trained conductor would. I look with great admiration, actually, at conductors who use nothing but the wrist and the little finger and come off stage without a bead of sweat and get into their Lamborghini.

And do you enjoy the process of throwing yourself into the music and the relationship with the players, and seeing what happens?

Well, some of the time it's thinking, 'Oh God, I still can't get this together because I didn't write it in the right way,' or, 'The phrasing in the second oboe is wrong and that's why I can't get it together.' That's what I think, because you always find another misprint. You always find another note too many that you've put in, all the time.

But you don't have to conduct it and you don't have to conduct anything at all, if you don't want to.

It gets me out of the house.

And you're more comfortable on the podium than in the audience?

Yes. And that's new.

When did that change?

I suddenly realised I was just a ball of nerves whenever someone else was playing my music. I think it was also possibly related to having reached a certain distance from the composition of an older piece, so with a piece that was, say, fifteen years old, suddenly I realised it was the past and I couldn't change it. It was like an old photo where you go, 'I can't believe I'm wearing that thing.' And that was a truthful reaction. And then I realised that the piece was more important than me; even something as unimportant as one of my pieces, I was even less important than it.

It explains why when I've seen you on stage, after a performance of your music that you haven't conducted – like in Berlin, at the premiere of Tevot *in 2007 – you look terrified.*

Well, you try going on stage at the Philharmonie. Besides, I was in Germany and I had written a piece with E flat minor in it and key signatures have been against the law there since the war because they make the Germans feel guilty, for some reason. I don't know why. I was terrified. I'm not thinking about how I look in that situation.

When I've seen you after you've conducted that piece, you turn round to the audience in a completely different way.

That may be because I'm too exhausted to think about where I am. This is something to learn. Performers should never think about even one hundredth of a second in the past. They should only ever think about the next thing. Great performers never look backwards. And you should do that in composing as well, in an ideal world. It's how to live. I cling to the hope that this can be achieved through learning and discipline. Some people are born with it. I also lack the gift of patience, which can be a real bore if you're a composer. Again, I think one can train oneself. But I find it difficult to distinguish between patience and entropy. Although there is a huge distinction.

How does that affect you as a performer, if you don't have patience?

You need it to practise. In combination with alertness and critical precision, it is the only way to improve. And also, when I'm working with other performers, in my own music, whether it's an orchestra or anybody else, they don't know my music as well as I do.

I've seen you in a rehearsal and you were very patient with orchestras.

Being polite is not what I'm talking about. In even the best performance, I hear only the gaping mistakes and lacks. A lot of the time I am only aware of the gulf between what I want and what I hear. To write music and to have it played are two different things, and some composers never recover from the shock. How lucky Beethoven was to be deaf! I'd give anything just to be able to switch off my ears and only hear through internal earphones, selectively. But it's one thing to write a chord for four instruments and quite another when four people sit down and play it. Then you've got four people involved. If you've got eighty people involved, it's twenty times more uncontrollable.

Do you sometimes wish your music could be realised without performers, for example as an electronic score?

I often wish I could make an object that would be the piece, some perfected electronic thing. The simple answer is, I don't know how to do it. I don't know how that works. Of course, I could learn. But I also don't know how it works expressively. It would feel like I was living as a form of radio waves, rather than as a human being. It's to do with the organic nature of somebody picking up an instrument and blowing or scraping it, and it makes a noise and it's your work. Also, electronic things break as a matter of course. And the technology is always changing, the models have a built-in obsolescence. But the violin hasn't changed for three hundred years, and more. When I'm writing, I work on an electronic keyboard with headphones. I don't write at the piano any more. This started to happen in the last ten years.

You make recordings on an electric keyboard?

Temporary recordings.

They're so you can listen back?

It's just a very crude tool for layering.

How long are those recordings?

A few seconds. I delete most of them as I go along, and all of them when I finish a piece.

Do you transcribe everything you record?

Of course not. What ends up on the page has barely any relation to these recordings.

Are you able to assign the notes to different instruments?

Yes, but the timbral quality of the sounds on the keyboard varies. The plucked sounds and the piano are bearable, but sustained things like strings, trumpets, oboes are of hideous quality. But I often deliberately use some kind of brutal ugly sound, because I don't want to confuse this sketch with the actual music. If I have composed a melodic vocal line or something, I will record it on a hyper-synthetic noise, some strident awful chemical noise, the exact opposite of what I want to hear, so that I can hear the reality of the notes more clearly.

In order that you don't get seduced by the colour?

I won't be seduced by the colour. It's so that I can hear the line in relief.

So it's a combination between writing things down and improvising?

I never notate improvisation. There may be some improvising coming in, but that is only at a very early stage, a rough model, a blob of clay in the crude shape of what the end result wants to be. You have to start somewhere. But as I work I gradually see the image more quickly. It was around the time I was writing *America* that I started using a minidisc recorder; I'd record a passage on the piano, to judge the perspective, as there were so many layers, and I wanted something very precise in perspective and not just a general noise. If I use the piano, it's to keep the perspective clear. I've tried working away from the piano to see what would happen, just to see, if at all, how the piano is affecting my writing, and I realised very quickly that without the piano the perspective went wrong. The piano was providing a clear perspective. It's not to do with the piano per se – it's just a tool. Anyway, writing *America*, I would record a passage at the piano, then listen to it and at the same time play another layer. It was very cumbersome, so I realised I needed to work on an electronic keyboard.

Would you ever be tempted to make electronic music?

Never say never. Though I doubt it.

Why?

I worry about equipment not working, fuses going, blackouts, that sort of thing. Also I fear it would not feel real to me. I would feel like Mike Teevee in *Charlie and the Chocolate Factory*, after he's been through the camera and he's just a pixel. I can't explain why. But the idea that what matters is the human aspect of the listener or the players, is wrong – that doesn't matter, on its own.

But you said it yourself: you just talked about 'the organic nature of somebody else picking up an instrument and blowing or scraping it'.

No. What doesn't matter is the humans in the concert hall, in terms of the listeners. Of course I'm writing for them in one sense. But it is not my job to worry about their experience. I don't care whether they hear something played by an iPad or by the Band of the Coldstream Guards. Maybe they actually love music. Maybe they care passionately about it. Maybe they are just there because somebody dragged them along. The point is, I can't know and it would be no use if I did. I only think about that in the vaguest sense.

So you don't worry about what kind of experience your listeners are having in the ten minutes or the two hours that you're making people sit through.

It was the time that was the point, not the people. Those are my ten minutes, my two hours. My part is to colour that time. I hate the word 'people'. When someone uses it they are usually lying about something for their own benefit. 'People want' this, 'people want' that. It's always an alibi, an excuse for something bad, something cheap, a shoddy compromise. I write for humans. Do you want to be thought of, when you are sitting in a concert hall, as 'people'? You're not 'people'; you're an individual. Caring for the time spent listening to one of my pieces has nothing to do with guessing the taste patterns of an audience. I'm talking about time as an abstract thing. I'm not thinking about the private responses of individual audience members. That would be presumptuous: how could I know what happens in other people's heads? My work is the only way I can try to understand what it might be like to be in someone else's head. When I'm writing music, I'm partly asking, 'Is it like this for you?' – but I'm not saying it to a particular person. It's a question that no-one can really answer: 'How does this sound to you?'

When you play a work by other people, sorry, composers, are you trying to recreate something primal about the composition of the work?

Well, I wish. Just as in an abstract sense, I know that there was a sound, an idea, before something was written on paper, so you have to be able, in a way, to rip up the score and throw it in the bin, because the score is just a map of intentions. The score isn't the thing. The music came before the score. And the music is the thing behind the surface. That's why I love Liszt. It's very clear in his music that there is a sound that the piano is making, even the piano in his head, or there was some magical thing happening in his ears when he sat down and produced those notes, long before he wrote them down and the piece materialised. And I think sitting down and playing them and writing them down were very close activities for him. That is why there is so much of it, almost as though he was carrying a little tape recorder around – the sheer volume, the vast productivity of the man. But I'm convinced that if you just sit down and play what it says on the score, you are not going to understand Liszt. You have to imagine that it is coming directly from his fingers and reinvent that moment when he wrote those three notes and they sounded completely new and fresh. A miracle. It can be recaptured and it should be recaptured. That's what the project of sitting down and performing a piece by Liszt on the piano should be: recreating the miracle of it being new. It sounds a grand claim, but obviously that should be the goal.

In your own playing, are you aware when you get close to this ideal? You must think, 'That was good. That was less good.'

Well, obviously. So many other things come into play: one can be distracted, for example. One has somehow to reduce the question of one's own state and mood at the time to the minimum – ideally nothing, no distraction.

So you're not thinking about whether you're hungry, thirsty, tired . . .

All of the above, no doubt. But those things have to be transcended, in order to have a hope of producing anything beyond mere reflexes.

Is this different for recording than for a live concert?

A recording is simply a document of that process in some other form. What I'm talking about is a thing that happens in the moment. It doesn't really matter if there is anyone in the hall.

You must feel differently if there are people there!

Not really. It's a wonderful thing if you've ever been fortunate enough to play alone in a great concert hall or a great cathedral or whatever it is, where there's nobody in it. That can be the most miraculous thing of all. It's simply a question of degree, whether it's three thousand or zero people listening. It doesn't affect whether you are going to achieve the transference I'm talking about.

So the reason you perform is to have an unqualified experience of music in the moment. Is that what you need, which the compositional process doesn't give you?

I think they're two sides of the same coin. For me, it's almost an acoustical thing, actually, because the acoustic in my head, the acoustic in my studio, is not the ideal acoustic that I'm imagining my music being heard in. It's completely dry. And that's not ideal.

But in the reality of performance, you're always going to face different and potentially challenging acoustics, aren't you, not the ideal?

You might face a completely vile acoustic, but there are other factors. When you put it in a concert hall, you're also actually putting it in the street, as it were. *Arcadiana*, my first string quartet, was once played in the open air, in Hyde Park in London. I loved it because the reality of the music was more apprehensible, the piece felt more real, with the traffic going past, the leaves rustling, people shouting and playing games in the distance, and particularly when a plane went overhead and you were suddenly aware that the music was a real thing, a living thing, as much as if it were someone talking. And the final movement, 'Lethe', seemed unnecessary in the open air because we already had around us what that movement represents, in some ways – the things that are outside my piece, going on, indifferent to it. In Hyde Park they were already part of the performance.

That living-ness – whether it's in Hyde Park or in a concert hall – isn't that why you don't just make recordings at home and release them, because you want your music to be a living thing?

But it's already living, in the score. It's like Ariel trapped in the tree. It's there. It's alive. Those Liszt pieces, the moment that only happened once, when he first heard those sounds, is alive in the score. It's captured there, because you're dealing with a master in that case. So I don't really see a distinction. Yes, perhaps, it does need a concert hall, a recording, whatever it is, to be released. I don't know. I don't care, actually. Maybe it doesn't. What have you got against deaf people? The thing is it's simply just not something I think about. It really isn't. It's so fundamental to me, I don't think about it.

I'm not trying to make you say anything about liking or communicating to 'people'; just that if you really wanted to do all those things, you've got any number of options, not just electronics, but other art forms, other media that you could be working with and aren't.

If I really wanted to do what?

If you really wanted to be a sound artist or an installation-ist or whatever.

But I am a sound artist. I think that's exactly what I am. I'm just doing it in a very much more elaborate way than someone who puts a microphone next to a tap. It's not for me to say which one's better, but it's the same thing. It's pure sentimentality to imagine that they're two different things.

But surely, the person with the microphone ends up with something which is always identical to itself, whereas one of your scores has infinite variables in live performance.

Yes, but I make the score as precise as possible. What happens in performance is separate – that's life, if you like. If the variable is the result of something I have written – like a balance that is unreliable, because I have used a marking in the strings which could mean 'very short' in America and 'quite long' in Germany, so in Germany you can't hear the singer for that second when I want you to hear them – then I will alter the score so that the marking can only be played very short, even in Germany.

Orchestra, solo piano, operas, they do make a journey with us through time. They travel through time. When you hear an orchestra playing a piece by Liszt now, it doesn't mean the same thing as an orchestra playing a piece by Liszt in the 1860s. It is a continuing miracle of the medium, that those things are refreshed over time. To take a more extreme example, from the eighteenth or seventeenth century or even earlier, you can't really know what it meant to sit and listen to those things played in the way that they would have been at the time. We have our own ways of doing it now, which would probably seem quite alien to people from that period. But it's part of the strength of notated music that it travels through time. But you see, if you take an early Beatles recording, you could write down everything that happened in it and reproduce it. You could get people to play that exactly as written. But it would not sound like the original. It would lack the atmosphere. Because the atmosphere is not notatable. It wouldn't be enough just to write it down. It would still not be an identical reproduction of the recording: to really get close to what it meant at the time, you would have to re-imagine it as new. That's what one's doing when one performs. It's an unsolvable problem to which one keeps returning. So when you perform a piece of nineteenth- or eighteenth-century music from score, you can try to recreate the original atmosphere in terms of today.

Let's take the case of performances where all the notes are in the right place – they still vary a lot.

Exactly. It's a responding to the temperature, I would call it, of the hall, which is to do with how many people are in, or its acoustical qualities. You could perform differently according to the city that you're in and the way things are felt there – your sensibility in New York, say, might be very different from that in Vienna – and according to the season, the year, the time, the place; all these could affect the atmosphere of the performance. If it's an intelligent and alive performance, it may take these things into account.

The question of tempo, for example, metronome marks – that's certainly not absolute. What they imply should be respected, but not, I think, to the exclusion of the reality of the place and time that you're in, and the instruments and the players that you're working with. One person's crotchet equals 118 might be another person's crotchet equals 96. It all depends on a lot of things. They are very dangerous things, metronome marks, but you can't really not have them. I am thinking of writing them in inverted commas. I've already used inverted commas for dynamics, often.

What does that mean?

If I write 'pp', it means: play to *sound* pianissimo. If it is a trumpet with a practice mute in, say, that might mean the player has to play what to them feels like fortissimo. But it is to balance with, say, a viola harmonic that is being played pianissimo elsewhere. Tempo too is relative. This is why metronomes are very dangerous, because tempo is not a question of beats per minute. The minute is a variable thing – in music, in lived experience. Minutes stretch and contract, depending on where you are or what's going on around you. A minute is not the same as another minute: in music it's not the same. A minute in New York is not necessarily the same as a minute in Lisbon; a minute in summer could be different from a minute in winter. A minute is fixed, on a watch, on a clock, but that's actually an artificial thing.

It's possible to be very specific now about the subtlest instructions to the players. Can you notate everything you want?

No. You can give as many clues, as many leads as possible, but nothing will work unless it is felt by the players. One can be more specific now than, say, Beethoven could, in terms of tiny subtleties of taking time here or there or of articulation; but in fact he or Berlioz or Wagner are also very specific, by their own lights, if you know the signs. I mean, the nuances of tempo, of hesitation and articulation in later Beethoven, especially, are very precise: the magnificent volatility of tempo and mood in the Op. 131 quartet, the precision of the gradations of tempo and decoration in the Op. 109 sonata. But the performer shouldn't do these things just because they are printed. I say this with both hats on.

Say a composer has written 'ritardando'. You don't just slow down because it is tells you to. The idea of the ritardando, the slowing down, was there in the music before he wrote the instruction. The reason for it being there is not just that he wrote it down. The music came first. So you must look for the reason why that ritardando has to happen, and then it will happen.

Now that the technology is available, do you ever want to make a fixed recorded version of something, and not bother with a score and performers?

It's tempting, but it is not in the nature of the music that I write to be fixed. It's not like a pop song, where the recording is the song. The alchemy of live performance is more elusive, because you might not get the magical effect more than one time in every ten. In fact, in classical music, say in the recording I've just been doing, if you do many long takes of a whole movement or a whole piece, they're going to have quite different characters. Your mood might have slightly shifted in five minutes in some way that then affects what you do with the balance of a chord or the exact timing of a rubato. You're still doing what it says on the page, but the variables are infinite. So when it comes to one's own music, there are infinite different ways of performing it while still sticking strictly to the score. I'd love to be able to have five or six or eight or ten different recordings of a piece of mine, because in most cases there's only one, so far, or maybe two – but those are not necessarily the best way to do it, certainly not the only way. And also, my music can be very risky, it's chancy. I don't intend it, I don't sit down and think, 'Let's make this as risky as possible' – that would be mad. But 'as safe as possible' often means 'very risky'.

Is this to do with virtuosity?

Of course it is connected to that. I think virtuosity is often very much undervalued. Even the way you ask that question makes the word sound as if it's held in a pair of tweezers. Virtuosity has been suspect for a while – it's said to be just 'for its own sake'. That's completely wrong. Virtuosity is higher than profundity, or beauty of sound, or giving a touching interpretation of an operatic role. Those are the things that are 'for their own sake'. Virtuosity pits the individual against failure. Virtuosity is in defiance of our fate, it is a very fundamental thing and if you have it, why would you hide it? I've been recording my piece *Lieux retrouvés*, for cello and piano, and what the cellist has to do, when I really watch the hands of the player, in the trio of the cancan, is leap over huge distances to land on a tiny little patch. It's athletic and musical at once. And watching, I realised in that moment that time had stopped in my head. Virtuosity is our victory over time, over extinction, in its purest form.

Has digital recording affected the way we see the virtuoso, now that almost any effect can be created in the editing?

In some ways, the collapse of studio recording, and the re-emergence of live recordings, is actually quite a refreshing opportunity to go back to a more natural, live virtuosity, particularly with larger things like orchestras and operas. I don't just mean playing fast: it's to do with precision, of which slow music demands just as much. I'm sure there will continue to be studio recordings, but there will also be more live recordings. Many orchestras now have their own labels: we're likely to obtain better quality than those terrible old live recordings we used to have in the Fifties, or whenever it was, but nor will it be that artificial studio sound that you and I largely grew up with.

Have you got a margin for error that you're willing or not willing to tolerate? Because you don't want a cautious approach, but equally, there comes a point when the thing is scarred by the difficulty of the technical demands?

Well, I think artists are always naturally pushing at the limits – to get anywhere you have to cut at some old wood.

Any composer will do the same, just by the nature of the way that one thinks: you're looking towards something or other beyond the horizon, so in order to get there you will probably be asking instrumentalists to do some things which have not necessarily been done before. It's in the nature of one's work. So in that, because you're dealing with other people, there'll be friction.

Do you listen to the advice of musicians? Might a demand that you've made ever be wrong?

Oh, of course I listen. And then you can ignore them, or not – absolutely you might be wrong in the precise way you tried to obtain the effect. There might well have been a better way. The same is true of every parameter. Tempo, or where the players sit, everything. You have to be prepared to make changes in practice that would have seemed impossibly huge when you were writing the piece. You realise: actually, this would work much better either much faster or much slower. You think of something at one tempo and it turns out that in fact in context that was not the right speed. And that can extend to timbre, volume, all sorts of things. The music itself does in some ways become quite fixed earlier – what the notes are going to be and the rhythm and all that – but to really get the most vitamins and nutrients out of the music, you have to be prepared to say: oh, this place should actually be half the speed. Or, the trumpets should stand in the audience, like in my *Polaris*. These are huge changes. Anyone who performs will be aware of the need for such flexibility.

Does that mean the ideas change? Is it a new idea?

No, it's that the way to extract full energy from the idea is not necessarily the way that you initially thought of. If one is sitting in a room on one's own, writing – perhaps I've had a lot of coffee, or I might be irritable or tired or whatever it is – those factors might mislead you as to the nature of the music you are writing. I have support for this at the highest level, because Beethoven, you know, used to drink coffee when he worked, and he was so obsessive about the exact strength of the coffee that he used to count out the beans one by one into the grinder. Now, that proves to me that he must have known from experience a number of beans that was too many and a number that was too few. I have my theories as to which pieces might have resulted from those respective situations. Now, very often, Beethoven's metronome marks are, to us, shockingly fast. Not all, but some are virtually unplayable – the first movement of Op. 106, for example, or of the 'Eroica'. Could it be that he felt the tempo in his head in a slightly altered way, because of some nervous response to circumstances, and didn't take into account the alternative physicality of live performance, performance in a space other than his own head?

I have had examples of this in my own work. There was one the other day when we were recording my cancan in *Lieux retrouvés*, and I thought, this is called *Cancan macabre*, it has to be fast. Now, there is only one cancan, Offenbach's cancan from *Orpheus in the Underworld*. It's a galop in genre, but it's *the* cancan. And I had this idea, to write a *cancan du diable*, because Liszt had written a piece called *Czárdás macabre*. Liszt in demonic mood is fascinating, because it's an irrational harmony. So I thought, why not write a *cancan macabre*. It's probably an absurd idea, but I did it and there it is. But with my cancan, if you played it at the speed of Offenbach's, it is too fast to feel the kicks. It should be like a row of cancan dancers with blades on their feet or something. It's a cancan of doom, cancan to the abyss.

But that meant that it had to be slower than you thought.

It had to be slower.

But was it slower when you did it in concert as well?

It was faster in my head when I was writing it, and in concert, but in the end, for the recording, it was slower. It was more itself with less speed. That's not the first time that's happened. The last scene of *The Tempest*, with Caliban alone on the island, I imagined as a dance. I wrote it as a dance, and I imagined it being fairly brisk. And I was orchestrating quite late, so they were rehearsing it without me, and they had that scene last. When I went into the opera house I heard it for the first time being sung, I thought: this is not at all how I imagined it, this is too incredibly slow. And they were so clear that this was right, because they'd been rehearsing the whole opera. When you're writing something you're crawling along a cliff wall. You don't see the whole cliff, obviously – but the cast had been seeing the whole thing, and they were very certain that it would be right to do the last scene slower. And I ultimately had to admit they were right. It was definitely the right tempo for it, although it took me ages to get the original speed out of my head.

A problem you face is that because you perform and have recorded so much of your repertoire, people regard your recordings as 'the composer's interpretation', and therefore as definitive documents.

That assumes I have all the skills to achieve what I want as a conductor or a pianist. Maybe I don't.

Do you think of your recordings as a reference?

Not a definitive one, no: they're just there as a marker, so people can hear what noise it's going to make, but there is no sense in which they're definitive.

But it's probably the way they're seen by others, in the way that say, Stravinsky's recordings are seen.

Well, that would be wrong, because he wasn't an especially good conductor, let's be honest about it. He was wonderful, a man of warmth, actually, in his performances. They're fabulous and often very beautiful, but it would be a mistake to think that they're authoritative, because he may not have had the technique as a conductor to achieve what he really wanted as a composer.

You've talked as composer and conductor interchangeably. With your composer hat on, you've said that when you write precise instructions you are not imagining the live performance . . .

. . . except in the vaguest, most abstract way – how can I, any more than the man who makes the cogs in a Ferrari can think about the car going round the track at 230 mph?

. . . whereas as a performer, you've said that you take the tempera-
ture of the hall, of the acoustic, into account when interpreting
the composer's directions. Does one inform the other?

Well, I write acoustics into my pieces, often. Like that
experience of 'Lethe', when I found out in Hyde Park that
'Lethe' functioned as the sound of a forest in a concert hall.
Similarly, in *Asyla*, I wrote the score so that it would contain
that sound that we live with all the time now: that electrical
hum or hiss, that sheen on the texture of life, especially in a
city, where it is inescapable but takes on so many different,
iridescent colours. I wrote that sound into the score, so that
it would have this electronic sheen. And in *Powder Her
Face*, I wrote the sounds of the eras into each scene – so that
the pre-war scene would have a Palm Court acoustic, the
sound of teatime at the Waldorf, say, with the noise of
spoons quietly hitting a hundred teacups; and the Fifties
scene the acoustic of a Paul Anka pop record, in a diner,
with those pizzicati and congas and the pop of the needle
on the '45' in a jukebox; and the Seventies scene would have
a transistor-radio noise, a tinny, psychedelic iridescence.
But this is not new. A good composer builds their own
acoustic. I try. I mean, the acoustic of Beethoven's Fifth is
that of a high hall with marble columns, hard and resonant,
the timpani echoed by the horns, the overhang of a violin
note, composed into the score; whereas the acoustic of the
Sixth is outdoor, rural, in the 'Scene by the Brook' – not just
the birds, you can hear the sound of water in the noise of
the hair of the bows crossing the strings, in the sound of the
fingers of all those left hands patting and releasing the
strings up and down, you can hear the leaves rustling. Or
the sudden change of acoustic at the end of the slow

movement of the 'Hammerklavier', Op. 106: for the final chord, which is marked softer than the one before, 'ppp' instead of 'pp', he removes the *una corda* pedal, so that it is as if the softer chord is played in a larger hall – as if suddenly a screen has vanished and revealed a vast nave behind the stage in which this quietest chord suddenly reverberates. So the acoustic is metaphorical and composed. That's how a composer thinks about the live performance, Tom. Not as an event, a social event, but as the revelation of a new world.

7

The Aldeburgh Festival – Haydn's hurdy-gurdy – Britten's operas – the suspect nature of 'perfection' – finding the 'inner music' in a new piece – the danger of reducing a work too far – the inexplicability of music

You directed the Aldeburgh Festival for ten years. How did you approach that?

I simply put on music that I like. I'd never done a job of any kind before and I wasn't interested in the social side of it, the concert as a social event – as you know. But it was a suitable festival for someone of that disposition, given that the founder, Benjamin Britten, was not by many accounts especially sociable. When I was about ten, I used to make programmes of piano music, writing the names of pieces I could play on a sheet of paper, covering the sheet. It was in the form not of a list, but a cloud, made of the names of pieces, each in its own little box. And I would present it to my parents and they would have to choose the piece that I would play. So I loved the mysterious things that would happen in the air when you, as it were, hung one piece next to another. I noticed also that to make an obvious pairing, a theme or a family connection, might paradoxically end up killing both pieces.

So in Aldeburgh my only criterion was my own pleasure. I hoped that would be a good barometer of everyone else's – and it was interesting, by and large. I put on, for example, a lot of Nancarrow: a great composer, very influential, very rarely on programmes for the simple reason that the vast majority of his works are for player-piano. So we presented some in the cinema, because to me it's a cinematic experience watching a mechanical piano, with nobody on stage, not a theatrical one. To show that mechanical music was not new, I put one Nancarrow study in a concert with a Haydn concerto for hurdy-gurdy, the *lira organizzata*. That was my first concert.

Well, I didn't listen to the Haydn *lira organizzata* concerto before I put it in. I just thought, this is going to be a piece by Haydn of that period. So I was not prepared for the shock in the concert. The theme is played genteelly by the strings, and then the hurdy-gurdy enters – and if the ceiling of the concert hall had fallen in I wouldn't have been more surprised by the noise. It was an unbelievably coarse, raucous sound. I'm sure the performer was wonderful – that is simply what the instrument is, there's nothing you can do about it. It plays a pedal note in the tonic, a C, at all times, no matter what key the music is in; throughout the slow movement, which is in G, the C was still sounding. Of course I loved it, but I was sitting amongst journalists, critics and whoever they were, and I could just see total, frozen horror. It was refreshing. I was also ecstatic, because this was the closest you could come to a recording of a sound from the eighteenth century, and it was, to modern ears, unacceptably crude, quite beyond the pale. And it made a point for me about the industry of playing and presenting music from the past, the whole sentimentality of that circus. That music is alive, kicking and screaming, not some shrink-wrapped heritage product.

But it also symbolised something quite profound: that something that you imagine to be familiar is completely, utterly strange. The other thing about Aldeburgh is the mantle of British music that it symbolises.

Oh, God, mantle, is it? That is not my concern. I don't think like that.

I know you don't. But what were your feelings about Britten's music at the time you began the job?

I liked Britten's operas when I first heard them, at fourteen, fifteen years old, which I think is the right time. In a way this may not be that fruitful as a question, because you're really asking me about something that did not turn out to be that central to me. I loved playing *The Turn of the Screw* at the piano, *A Midsummer Night's Dream*, and *Peter Grimes* a little less. They had just the right combination of astringency and tenderness for me at that age. *Billy Budd* was too ugly for me then: I liked it slightly later, maybe seventeen, when I was reading Forster, but went off it quite quickly. But at the same time as I was discovering these operas of Britten, I was listening obsessively to *Façade*, and also to *The Soldier's Tale*, in English, of course, and playing the percussion parts along with the record. And that was love, as it turned out, because ten years later, when I came to write an opera, the DNA turned out not to be from Britten, but from those other directions, along with operas from other countries.

How, then, did you approach the question of Britten's music in the Aldeburgh Festival?

Naturally, with enjoyment, because I had much admiration for his music and for what he had done. Of course, I steered things in a certain direction, because I preferred some of Britten's pieces to others, as anyone would. I was always thrilled to have performances of the *Missa brevis*, or *Our Hunting Fathers*, or the Violin Concerto. Whether every page of every opera was completely at the top of my personal Parnassus is irrelevant, really. Although I did flee screaming from the hall when we had the Aldeburgh premiere of *Peter Grimes*, because I just couldn't stand it.

Why not?

It became apparent to me why Britten had not wanted it performed there. It's so mean about the people of Aldeburgh. They're all madams or paedophiles or small-minded maniacs, and meanwhile the real people of Aldeburgh were all sitting there around me, and they didn't look like that at all. They seemed perfectly normal. I find that an embarrassing opera from start to finish.

Why?

I don't believe it.

Why: because you don't believe the drama, you don't believe the story, you don't like the music?

I don't terribly care about this man. I don't think it's a very good subject for an opera. It's a little bit thin. It's a good idea for an afternoon radio play or something, this little sad thing that happened, but it's not *Wozzeck*, is it? It wants to be. It doesn't have universal grandeur. It's like watching a TV drama. It starts in the courtroom, then we have the scene setting. It seems a bit 'by numbers' to me. It's *Wozzeck*, but on rationing. It's as though he wanted it to be *Wozzeck* but he didn't have enough coupons. It's not rich enough for me. It's impoverished. You may not feel that. Maybe I just have rich tastes. For me *Albert Herring* is much more successful, the marriage of Britten's musical genius and the tone of the piece. The threnody, or whatever it's called, in *Albert Herring*, when they think he's died but he hasn't, is perfectly judged. The balance is exactly right, and it is much more moving than anything in *Peter Grimes*. I just can't believe in all these people dressed up as fishermen and that woman singing about her knitting. I mean, who cares? You might care. I know it's a big thing where you come from, knitwear.

But can you understand why people will be surprised to hear you say that?

No. Why?

Well, because people like it: opera houses, conductors, singers, performers, audiences love this piece.

That's nothing to do with me.

What I'm really keen to talk to you about in terms of Britten is what you learn or don't learn from his example in terms of opera-writing. As a composer writing operas in English, surely you can't escape his legacy?

Why not? There's a very simple problem with Britten for me, which is the problem of singing in English. It's not a problem in Handel, it's not a problem in Purcell; in fact it's magnificent in Purcell. The way that the emotion, the rhythm of the words, is rendered into the music is incomparably natural and powerful. Now, when you move to Britten, I don't think it's a problem with the quality of the libretti or of the music. It's that the music does not match the everyday English phrases coming across. There is something unnatural in the relationship between the words and the music. It's hardly surprising, he was doing something quite new.

You're talking about a kind of vernacular in Britten.

It's problematic. When I listen to Puccini I'm not aware of any embarrassment over the way he uses vernacular phrases. That may be because I don't speak Italian.

What is the embarrassment with Britten, and do you have it with other operas in English? Tippett, for example?

Well, I don't have it with Tippett, because there's an artificiality to the words in Tippett; but that is supremely the case in Stravinsky's *Rake's Progress*, which is the best opera in English. There's a distance from conversational English in the way that the language is set in that piece, which removes the problem for me completely – because the music is also distanced, the relationship is natural.

But you can't describe the libretti in, say, Britten's Turn of the Screw *or* Death in Venice *as conversational English, can you?*

The problem for me is not the words, it's the combination of them with the music. The music makes it too conversational. It's too informal. It's just too much like people singing a bad play in English, to me. The music does not lead enough. It's simply not my taste.

You have never liked it?

I used to listen to it. I used to enjoy the percussion writing, when I was studying percussion, I must have been in my teens.

But in terms of artificiality, The Turn of the Screw *could hardly be a more formal opera.*

No, that's an entirely superficial view. That's a very common mistake. It amazes me that you are taken in by that.

OK – so what do you think of as formal? – because I want to get the definition of that right. When I describe The Turn of the Screw *as 'formal', I mean there is a serial theme and variations. But what you mean by 'form' in that sense is something very different. You're talking about a kind of animating life force or something running through, a reason for the notes existing. In other words, you don't mean 'form' in terms even of a structure, but something else?*

I see form as arising from content. Not just this game of 'Let's have a structure', which is dilettantish. I feel Britten puts that structural scheme in *The Turn of the Screw* so that critics or whoever could say 'Ah, structure!' and feel that they are in on the joke. That's what a British critic, forgive me, would think. It makes them feel clever, people who swallow and regurgitate received ideas but don't look at what they mean. It's a decoy, a veneer. In contrast to the formal things in Berg's *Lulu*, which are so transcended and overgrown that they cease to advertise themselves. But they give such depth to *Lulu*. That's real power. It's not fair to compare such things. But in *The Turn of the Screw* the formal conceits only show up the one-dimensionality of the piece. It's embarrassing that the title tells you exactly what the music is going to do. That's hobbyish.

Are there any other English-language operas that you enjoy?

Dido and Aeneas. I don't know. But my favourite piece by an English composer is *Façade*. Opera is a very strange genre. It is a perverse thing, to go and sit there and watch this morbid thing happen, sung. All great nineteenth-century operas have something grotesque, freakish about them. In the twentieth too: *Wozzeck* – freakish, *Lulu* – freakish, *The Rake's Progress* is quite freakish, with its bearded lady and devil and lunatic asylum. It's the maddest thing to do in the 1950s, to write this eighteenth-century pastiche – pastiche is not the right word, but whatever *The Rake's Progress* is – charade, perhaps. Britten's subjects are slightly mundane by comparison. They are all very explicable, which the English like, God help us. They are too explicable. Too literary, perhaps. You're not really looking at works of art, though, because of it.

What are you looking at, then, for goodness' sake?

Ersatz.

You can't mean that. Does none of your teenage feeling for the music remain?

I went to see *A Midsummer Night's Dream* recently, looking forward to being disturbed by it as I was at fourteen. It used to arouse a world of troubling feelings in my stomach. It seemed to suggest so much. And perhaps I've changed, because although the music has some very beautiful things in it, I found it too one-dimensional.

But surely what he does in that piece is offer you a world of humans and a world of spirits, each successfully characterised in the music.

That is precisely the problem. The music is too pat. The ideas go nowhere. You lift them up and there's the floor. It's like a school play.

What would make it less superficial?

You honestly can't tell the difference between that and something with any depth, with three dimensions in the music? The material does not develop – it is simply repeated, expanded, contracted, but does not develop. It doesn't connect to itself. It's like dried flowers. Take the motifs, for example. I get the feeling he's just discovered them that morning and jotted them down over breakfast. They don't have a chance to grow into one another.

He did write that piece very quickly.

Evidently. When I went to see it last year, the many delicious things in it, they faded, turned to ashes in my mouth, in my ears, as it were, because I realised it's a string of very thin ideas one after another. And the lovers' music is prefab. There is something 'Let's make an opera' about the whole thing. What you've done is lead me to talk about something that is not that central to me. I mean, I can clearly see how brilliant it is. Of course it is. I love much of the earlier Britten, mostly without words.

That would suggest, then, that when Britten doesn't write words, your relationship with his music ought to be much closer.

I am more comfortable. Even the *Serenade*, for example, is a bit embarrassing, although it's masterly. There's not a note out of place.

What's embarrassing about it, then? The words could hardly be more artificial.

Well, in *A Midsummer Night's Dream*, I get embarrassed by this idea, 'Here's a famous speech by Shakespeare, let's make a nice tune and set it to that.' It doesn't go deep enough. In the *Serenade*, they're famous poems – again, it's 'Let's set this famous poem, let's find the perfect image.' It's too obvious. I want it to be less perfect. The perfection is suspect. But the Violin Concerto, say, is fantastic. It flirts with danger, indeed goes beyond flirting. It takes huge risks, and better still it may not even quite get away with all of them – so you feel that you've gone on a three-dimensional journey from beginning to end, that he suffered fruitfully to find it. And the perfection in something like the *Missa brevis*, or *A Ceremony of Carols*, is exactly suited to the subject, so you feel it very powerfully. They have this fierce, almost angry precision, which is powerful in these delicate children's pieces with their slight primness. I don't feel that fruitful tension in the operas. The operas explain themselves too much. They give a polite account of themselves and write a nice legible thank-you letter to you. So when the sailors mutiny in *Billy Budd*, they do it quite politely. It's not enough to say, 'I feel like writing an opera on *Billy Budd*' and you write a sailor's chorus and that's enough and it works. To me it doesn't work. It's not animated.

Surely, the whole point about what animates those operas, and indeed much of his music, is the tension between the individual, the outsider, and a community, Britten's perennial preoccupation.

Well, isn't that nice.

It ought to mean, therefore, that he is suffering for it and it should at least have an emotional authenticity.

Not necessarily.

I'm saying that that's what people hear in his music, that tension between individuals and communities.

That's social life, that's private life. I don't care about that. I'm looking at you with disbelief because I can't believe you would say something so absolutely fundamentally stupid to me.

What, the idea that someone's life gives an automatic authenticity to their work?

That's the most ridiculous idea I've ever heard. It's actually insulting to Britten. Why would he take so much care with the facture of these works, which is very painstaking in some ways, if it would have had automatic authenticity even without that, because of some plot similarity with his personal circumstances?

What was your ambition in writing The Tempest, *then? It sets a Shakespeare story, after all, like* A Midsummer Night's Dream.

I'm absolutely not going to compare myself to Benjamin Britten.

That's not the point. I'm not asking you to compare yourself to Benjamin Britten. But you just said that it's not ambitious enough to get a speech of Shakespeare and set it to music.

No. I was very specific. I said it would be naff to take a famous passage and set it, verbatim, to a pretty tune. I don't take famous speeches from Shakespeare and put a pretty tune to it, in *The Tempest*. I don't take the famous text at all. It would be half-timbered, mock Tudor, which I find a bit in *A Midsummer Night's Dream*. The music ought to have some reason for existing beyond the fact of us all sitting down and deciding to set this play verbatim to music.

What, then, is the animating force in The Tempest?

I'm not suddenly going to go from talking about Benjamin Britten to talking about my own opera. I understand enough about the way I built that piece to know that it doesn't belong, musically, to the same genetic family as Britten. The aim was essentially to write a symphonic opera, which means that in theory the evening is driven by the musical logic at least as much as by the logic of the drama itself. That is simply a different genetic family from Britten. The DNA is not related. It's probably not even something he would have considered important.

You don't share a common ancestor in Berg?

Well, Berg had a lot of unofficial children. It is very nineteenth-century in some ways, *Wozzeck*, but I think that's what makes it all the more telling for us now. If something is looking in both directions that might actually make it stronger. To see looking backwards as a weakness is the kind of irrelevant moral judgement that somebody in the late twentieth century would make. Someone – a man who used to run a major opera house, whom I will not name – actually went on the radio and said how 'nineteenth-century' he thought *The Tempest* was because it has a chaconne, infallibly picking the one century in which chaconnes barely feature at all.

Something you said about Britten relates to a problem that you have identified in the past with your own music, which is that when things seem to be 'perfect', that's an impulse you recognise but try to resist.

Well, perfection is the right direction – but the destination itself may not be that interesting, once you arrive. Perfection can even be a cop-out, a substitute for deeper investigation. It is the right direction, of course, but it does not necessarily guarantee anything, if the thing that is perfected is itself nothing much. For example, whether *Lulu* is perfect or not is irrelevant. It probably is, but it couldn't matter less: for of all *Lulu*'s great qualities, perfection is the least important. *Lulu* is much better than perfection. The opposite might sometimes be true with a great composer like Britten – there can be a perfection which is more a limitation than a strength. Imperfection might have been better. But in all events when you're working the impulse is, 'I need to perfect this,' and much more time is spent honing things down than building things up. The pieces with the fewest notes in are probably the ones that took the longest. That's almost always true in my case, at any rate.

Do you mean the shortest pieces?

No, exactly not, I mean the most stripped down. The impulse is to reduce something to its simplest form, to make it as simple as possible. All pieces should be as short as possible and as simple as possible. That doesn't necessarily mean they will be short or simple.

I remember being surprised when I saw the finished score of The Tempest *that much of it was so pared down, whereas your sketches were piles of blackened pages.*

I recall the impulse when writing that piece was to reduce any thought to its simplest whole form. You might manage to do it, but then it's possible that if you reduce it too much, you lose something essential. It's as if there's a person you never met, you just read their obituary. Because you can reduce someone to just a few lines or whatever it is, and think that is all you need to know, but you haven't met the person, you haven't experienced their reality. You've explained them without knowing them. That's a danger with over-honing what you say in music, or in anything. One doesn't want to reduce it beyond its point of logical indefensibility – one doesn't want it to be explicable. Music should be inexplicable.

Is that when you know a piece has finished, in a way, when you have that sense that things are in that kind of balance?

Sometimes you don't have a sense. Some things just are finished. But then I look at it, I immediately start to see the things that are not there, and I sometimes need to restrain myself from going back into a piece and hacking away at it. But I trust the moments where you can feel it has come full circle and there is a sort of click. More and more I go through and make a long sketch of something, a long first draft, because one of the things with a long piece is that you're trying to find the inner music in it. That's one of the things I find a little bit missing in Britten's operas, an inner music.

By which you mean?

There's a music inside the piece that has its own consciousness, that I am not necessarily aware of until I've got quite a long way into it.

What is that? Is that a kind of Schenkerian reduction?

No, it's the complete opposite of that. It's why Schenker is wrong. It's all the things that are not in a Schenkerian reduction that have actually led to the piece being the way it is and not another way. He is a scientist who fails to understand that the life force was there before it entered a certain form. The form is a result of the inner music. So to hear the inner music I often go right through, very quickly, and listen from beginning to end, and I will start to notice that there's a connection between things.

Connection between chords, connection between moments, these are technical things?

It's all technical.

Fetish notes? That is, specific pitches that keep returning?

Yes, that might be a key that unlocks that door. It might be a note that recurs, or anything that connects. The connection occurs almost like a biological event and I suddenly realise that something has outlined a huge shape that wasn't planned. I come across that often. More and more, I keep finding connections, especially in longer pieces, that I'd never noticed during the composition. For example, there are words that are set to exactly the same notes at the beginning and end of *Powder Her Face*: the words 'Hold me' in the gramophone tune in Scene 2, and 'Hold me' at the end of Scene 8, are set to the same notes, in an unrelated context, and I wasn't aware of it when I was composing it. That is a clue, a key. But usually it's only at the last stage, when I'm making a final draft, that these things start cropping up, if I'm lucky, like rabbits jumping out of the ground, and circles start closing themselves all over the place. It's a magical but also a dangerous moment, because if I'm not careful I can take it too far and destroy the unpredictability, the indefensibility – and lose the piece and start writing the obituary.

Because at precisely that point –

It starts to solidify.

And if you start to close everything off too neatly, you actually reduce its power?

You can watch it solidifying, like a jelly setting, and you have to be careful at that moment, because there's a danger of it becoming flat, whereas to work it's got to have friction in it, in order to give a chance for things to spawn underneath the music and perhaps unmask some intention too deep to be aware of at a controllable level. Music should be inexplicable and indefensible.

8

first inspirations – the animating life force of Kurtág and Ligeti – the red herring of microtonal harmony – the discovery of irrationally functional harmony – the galvanic shock of Gerald Barry – burning an opera in the sink – patterns, spirals and serialism – Meredith Oakes's libretto for The Tempest *– the world in A major*

What were your earliest encounters with music?

Chopin – the first thing I wrote down, I think, was a tune that I found moved me in some strange way, like a very emotional memory of the mountains. And I realised afterwards that it was from the middle section of Chopin's first Polonaise – a haunting idea that seems to circle around itself in the air. These were all things from my parents' record collection – Chopin Polonaises, a record of flamenco, a record of songs from the Sephardic and Middle Eastern Jewish world, Paul Robeson, Joan Baez ... In terms of classical music, I have a feeling I started, as it were, in the middle, with Tchaikovsky and Smetana and Grieg, and worked outwards from there: forwards to Stravinsky, and backwards to Beethoven.

There were two large boxed sets of orchestral music which I lived in for years. It was a ripely mixed selection, with Brahms's Third Symphony – still by far my favourite – and *The Rite of Spring*, jostling with things like Flotow's *Martha* overture, Weber's *Invitation to the Dance* (in the

Berlioz orchestration), Smetana's *Vltava*, which led me on to the rest of *Má vlast* – that became my favourite piece. I still think of *Má vlast* as somehow the ideal piece of music. At my grandmother's house were chamber music records, the 'Trout' Quintet, and *Petrushka* and *Firebird* which I think I knew well before hearing *The Rite*. I listened a lot to Tchaikovsky's First Piano Concerto. These pieces all had physical dimensions to me: I didn't feel them as music, I felt them as landscape. The Tchaikovsky was mountainous. It wasn't a landscape simply depicted during the course of the piece. *Vltava* was that – more, I was very affected by the idea of the river passing through different landscapes: that moved me very much, the trickle at the beginning containing such potential and yet being so modest, almost regretful, about its destiny, and the passage that seems to depict fairyland with a castle or whatever it is affected me enormously. But the Tchaikovsky concerto, that was a vertical landscape as well. The noise that the first chord in the orchestra made, that particular chord, had an absolute physical presence for me, not simply as a mountain, but as all the furrows, the shadows, the valleys and the ledges, in every detail. The Brahms Third Symphony is a cliffscape, complete with gulls.

I had a bad start with opera. I saw *Carmen* on the television and was horrified to see him stab her at the end. It was a visceral shock. I instinctively knew that the music was saying the bull was being stabbed inside the ring at the same time. And not just the stabbing, the knowledge that she was being punctured, but the contrast of that terror with the bright, brilliant music traumatised me. I was inconsolable. I must have been about six or seven.

What was your first encounter with avant-garde music?

I remember getting the piano music of *Mikrokosmos* from the library and feeling almost physically sickened by the dissonances in 'From the Diary of a Fly'. It was a similar distress to the first time I heard *The Rite*, or, after that, *Symphony of Psalms*. I felt bilious. Messiaen came as an avalanche when I was about thirteen, probably. I loved the bird pieces first, because I was – am – a little bit ornithological, and then *Turangalîla* was a pillaging. The extremity in both directions – brutalism and sweetness. I was listening to Boulez and Stockhausen's music at the same time as I was discovering Britten's operas. Stockhausen seemed like a kind of aberration, a freak growth that had happened. Even then I felt aware that it wasn't, somehow, necessary. But I used to listen to *Stimmung* when I was about fourteen.

Did you enjoy it?

Yes, I did. I thought it was funny, and I liked the warm soupy harmony, but then the more I looked into the music of Stockhausen the more I felt it just seemed like a flower that had died months before and was still on the shelf in a vase. There was no animating musical life in it that I could detect. It was a theoretical thing, but there was nothing inside it musically to enjoy. It just seemed to me to be dead and desiccated. But of course, people who knew him would perhaps feel very differently. The only piece I can imagine myself enjoying now is *Kreuzspiel*, which has a kind of beatnik grooviness.

I listened to *Licht* as the instalments came out but I

just didn't feel the notes had an interesting relationship with each other that would be fruitful for me. It seemed to be driven more by some kind of dilemma that he'd got himself into, that he was born into, that he'd emerged into, whatever it was, some artistic conundrum, which was no longer present for me as a fifteen-year-old in the mid-Eighties. German post-war guilt, perhaps, or the denial of it, I don't know. So that didn't have much relevance to me, musically or otherwise. It seemed to me that the only thing that mattered was that he had theoretically to dominate; it didn't especially matter how. And that, to me, is uninteresting. The same feeling, slightly, stays with me about Boulez, although I was more struck by the actual music, but tended to feel generally the works were unnecessarily long. I still do, actually. I can't say they had, how shall I put it, irresistible allure.

Of the music of the generation born in the Twenties, you did respond to the music of Kurtág, in precisely that sense of the way the notes related to one another, didn't you?

That was an immediate reaction, in the bloodstream.

What was the piece that you first heard?

Messages of the Late Miss R. V. Troussova. It was played to me by Erika Fox at Junior Guildhall, so I would probably have been fourteen or so. And I can't explain what it was but I was instantly conscious that it was alive in every sinew: every note was a blood cell, carrying oxygen. At that point I wasn't particularly aware of what the problems or 'issues' might be in composition, in music. I knew there were some, I just felt they didn't refer to me. Perhaps I was already instinctively detaching myself. I just heard the sound of the woman singing and the cimbalom and was completely thrilled.

That piece, *Troussova*, is from the Seventies, so that would have been one of the very first pieces of absolutely recent music that I would have heard. And of course I immediately started trying to imitate it in some way and got it completely wrong. Yet it can be a way to start, to try to imitate and realise that you're not that person.

But in looking into the music of Kurtág, presumably you explored how he created this bloodstream of his music?

I made a study of it, yes. I felt the gestures had a real emotional life of some kind. They weren't theoretical. I wanted to discover how they seemed to be real human gestures, to have the power and energy of an actual fist coming down or a hand stroking.

Had you discovered something in Kurtág that the other music of the mid-century avant-garde didn't have?

I wouldn't have been aware of that at the time, but there was a dryness to other music around that time, a technical dryness and almost a conscious and deliberate lack of warmth. Actually, I invented a polarity between the two Hungarians – Kurtág and Ligeti – and came down on the side of Kurtág. I decided that of the two, Kurtág's was the

human, warm voice and Ligeti's was cold. I now see this
was wrong.

Why?

I persuaded myself that Ligeti had a sort of Stalinist attitude
– almost – to a single note, that it's one of millions and it
doesn't matter whether it lives or dies; it's just clay to him,
dead material. Whereas with Kurtág, the note is individual
and is a living, breathing thing and each one is vitally
important and must be nurtured – I felt more attracted to
that approach. That was what I thought at the time. But
then, of course, you go through and you realise that it's
more complicated than that. They start from a place that is
very close – in life, literally, and as artists. I now wouldn't
emotionalise the question in quite the same way. They
approach the problem, the predicament, from different
points of view, Ligeti perhaps cosmic, Kurtág more
intimate. I would see that in both cases you had inventors of
genius, inventors of colours and instruments – not in the
sense of actual musical instruments, but an 'instrument'
being a complex of timbre and interval and harmony
and rhythm, which could be an implement that you could
use, if you like, to inject the idea. They both invented
these new 'instruments', for very different purposes;
although as often happens they grew closer together.
Ligeti's *Síppal, dobbal, nádihegedüvel*, one of his last pieces,
is my favourite. And as it happens it starts to get quite close
to a Kurtág-like art. They're very short songs, in which the
percussion accompaniment is very closely linked to the
gestures of the voice. That's very like Kurtág. And I think
it is Ligeti's finest work, really. For me, it's the one I find

most moving, most perfect. He moved through all the alienation and trauma and arrived back at something really quite childlike, human at the end. If a great composer adumbrates the era in some way, Ligeti was a great composer. He was the first to bring the heat death of the universe into music, the idea of total entropy. His pieces are all tending in that direction.

Pieces like the piano Études as well as the Requiem, say?

Absolutely. I think that tends to be the vanishing point of any piece by Ligeti: the heat death of the universe. They have a sort of total cosmic despair, an absurdity about them, which is an entirely late-twentieth-century thing.

Even the miniatures?

Especially. He sets one of those piano Études going and it's going towards extinction from the moment it starts. That's what is in the material, and it was in him too, I think.

You mean the way those pieces set up patterns of rhythm and pitch that spiral out of control and into the infinite. Technically you could say that your own music does similar things, in a way, like that gigantic quasi-series at the end of Tevot, *which you've also described as something that could go on for ever, which could be infinite.*

But that's not quite the same, because it doesn't go towards extinction. Ligeti's ones have a vanishing point and mine don't. I could think of so many examples in his music. Take the first piano Étude, *Désordre*, for example – but almost all of his music has this vanishing point. And because it is so humanely done, there's something so moving about it. This becomes a human thing. There's a song in *Síppal* about the rickshaw driver, the coolie, which uses a vanishing spiral like that, '*kuli, kuli, kuli*': this man whose existence is totally without meaning and he's desperate, but he can't escape it. What could be more late-twentieth-century? And it's wonderful because it's also funny and, of course, the glorious thing about Ligeti is that there is all that ultimate despair, but it's also like a black cartoon joke. More importantly, he was also one of the first of that generation to really come back to dealing with triadic harmony and diatonic harmony in a way that I think bewildered some people at first. Although actually Kurtág was almost there first, in fact, in the *Játékok*. And indeed Conlon Nancarrow was there too, though he was doing it in total isolation then.

As usually happens with pioneers, Ligeti did not fully work through this seam, even within his own parameters. In my opinion. I mean to me one of the limitations in Ligeti is how he dealt with tonality when he started to think about diatonic harmony again. For example, the Horn Trio, the piece where that really starts to happen, has this very frivolous side. But to me the joke is too sweeping. Why are we here, dealing with this, if it's all just a black joke?

Do you think that's what Ligeti thought in 1982 when he wrote the piece, and caused all that fuss for those German composers who heard it as a regressive step, because of its quasi-tonality?

I was thrilled by the passion of the noise and the neon colour of the harmony. It seemed to me a genuine discovery, so actually I think that the blowing-a-raspberry side to it, the mockery, is less convincing than it was in the earlier pieces when there is very little functional harmony, like the Requiem. But then the Horn Trio is a very offensive piece; it would really have been heard as very offensive at the time.

But it was only really offensive to the avant-garde.

Oh no, all round, I think. It was offensive to the avant-garde not only because it used these forbidden harmonies, but because it did so in an avant-garde context, on their turf. It was a very conscious attempt, I believe, to create a diatonic harmony again. But it's a harmony that is also likely to offend traditional ears as improper. It's also a brilliant provocation and, from that point of view, a triumph. You can't just ignore something like that. You have to look at it. So I did, and thought, 'Well, actually, now we're dealing with these intervals, why don't we look at dealing with them more functionally, on their own terms, rather than so much as a provocative joke?' A sense of genuine dealing with intervals is very elusive to him in the piece. It tends to fragment because of the violence of the irony. I wanted it less fragmented. I suppose I wanted to create an irrationally functional harmony, in which the function is not only on the surface, but at a structural level. And try to make something that was not merely ironic or alienated, but also truthful. It could still be a sceptical music, in Wallace Stevens' phrase, but it would be real. To try to bring it back to real life in some way, back to the world.

Because there's also something almost disturbingly other-worldly about a lot of the music of Stockhausen, Boulez, Nono, at the top of the list. There's something very alienating about that music, rather frighteningly divorced from earth, I felt. At fifteen, twenty, you're conscious of this as a question: 'What is this? What is this noise? Is it in the world around me? No.' The simple fact is that that music uses the language of a horror film or a space movie, just in terms of the everyday. You could argue that isn't the point, but in fact that was the noise the avant-garde was ending up making, for everyone except about fifteen people. So that was also something one had to deal with. Is there a way through? Maybe not, but one had to try. When you're twenty you can try anything, but it wouldn't have fitted me for long, that alienated, other-worldly avant-garde hat. I need a bigger hat.

One thing you haven't explored, one of the things that Ligeti used, is natural tunings, quarter-tones and microtonal harmony.

Well, in fact I have, a little, but for Ligeti, I wonder if that was something of a red herring, a cul-de-sac, really. The Snark was a Boojum. Do you know the end of *The Hunting of the Snark*?

No.

Oh, it's a terrifying thing. He is hunting the Snark and someone says, 'Beware ... if your Snark be a Boojum ... you will softly and suddenly vanish away.' He finds the Snark and he catches the Snark, and he softly and suddenly vanished away, for the Snark was a Boojum, you see. Chilling. Of course, Ligeti was very interested in that universe of Lewis Carroll. Anyway, microtones: well, it's a wonderful colour to me, something like the opening of the

Violin Concerto, like going down a rabbit hole to find this colour. It's microscopically fascinating. But to me, it's still just a colour. It's perfectly possible that great music will be written, as maybe it already has been written, with quarter-tones. I love the mad acidic colours of the natural horns in Ligeti – they make me think of the colours of a wall covered in different graffiti – and also that effect that you get in some modern artists who use a mixture of graffiti spray paint and very acrylic things with normal oils and other media, and you get these strange perspectival effects. That's what it's like. But still, it's really just a colour. And he achieves similar perspectival effects with equal-tempered harmony.

I recently heard a performance of one of Ligeti's early harpsichord pieces that you can play on a mean-tempered instrument. It's a fantastic effect. *Passacaglia ungherese*. But I don't think that turned out to be a big way forward. I haven't seen yet how quarter-tones could be a way forward at a structural level. I have used it as an effect, as a background – like the quarter-tone detuned piano in *Asyla*. You can obtain a strong perspective. But it's not yet really a motor for driving a structure. When somebody works out how to do it, maybe it could be. I think there'll be a part of us which always feels it's actually just a kind of futuristic colour effect or ethnic inflection. In my case it was not futuristic or ethnic, it was to create a feeling of hearing the orchestra, if you like, through blurred ears, in some way, without any blurring of the image itself.

Is this irrationally functioning harmony something you find other precedents for?

Well, certainly it was present in Berlioz.

Berlioz creates an irrationally functional harmony?

Yes.

Through a different way of thinking about diatonic relationships?

Oh yes, exactly. Where, for example, the most irrational chord to use would be the tonic root position. In 'Le Spectre de la rose', he does that and it's so shattering. The tonic is used as a dissonance. It is undermining, utterly improper, and it's the tonic. It makes you feel somehow you're in wherever you are, but at the same time you're in a place far away from it. It's a profound effect. Even in the melody of the first allegro of *Symphonie fantastique*, the *idée fixe*, you have that. You see, Berlioz was really the first composer who had no harbour in sight, the first that gives no confidence that there is a great gate that the piece will finally steer through, like, say, Beethoven gives. In Berlioz the building is there, but the cement has disintegrated between the bricks. But it is a very interesting time, because meanwhile the harmony must still function. So the harmony functions, but irrationally: it is like the logic in Lewis Carroll.

Part of the power of this irrationally functional tonality is a primal thing. Everyone can recognise there is some mysterious charge of energy that happens when you move from I to V, from the tonic to the dominant, or from V to I, some magnetism that makes it appear that the two harmonies have an internal relationship, that creates that effect of one solving the other. But in fact, once you have realised that this is not necessarily inevitable, as Berlioz discovered in *Symphonie fantastique*, you can't go back.

Where else do you find this irrationally functional tonality?

Chopin, Liszt, Tchaikovsky, in a small way Grieg and Schumann. I think it was probably one of those things that was discovered, and wasn't recognised as a discovery, because it didn't stick out as a modern idea, a bomb through the building. It just sounded like something eccentric, a solecism, technical naivety. The things in Berlioz that were more obviously ruptures – the orchestral effects, harmonics, the multiple timpani, the distorted textures, the grotesquerie – all that blinded people to how innovative his use of tonal harmony was. For 150 years no one really saw that it was a discovery, that it was when he was at his most superficially conventional that he was seeing the furthest distance. And we went, in some ways, backwards. Progress was made, but with a crucial piece missing.

Who missed it, then? Is it something you find in Brahms or Strauss or Wagner?

I think Brahms is rather the opposite, seeking to bring wider harmonic circles back to heel within the symphonic argument. Strauss plays with things like that in a semi-erotic way, a titillating misplaced tonic. Ravel, especially in the late works, has it. In things like the Violin Sonata, it is there, in the opening of the slow movement, where the simple tonic–subdominant–dominant in the violin sounds like the most acidulous dissonance, extraordinarily penetrating.

Is it in Debussy?

The thing is with Debussy that he's very furtive. He's very sly. He'll disguise things. I heard that he was a kleptomaniac. If people had Debussy to dinner, they had to count the spoons. I mean something like the opening of the first piano Étude is an unusually bold case of it.

Why wasn't it heard? Why wasn't this irrationally functional harmony picked up?

It's not that it wasn't heard. It just wasn't recognised as a usable stepping-stone further across the river. Sometimes something can be not recognised as a stepping-stone until all the other paths have been tried and one has to go back and start from another path.

Does it have a prehistory even earlier than that?

Of course.

Something you were saying about fourths in medieval music?

Of course, the fourth, that has changed its meaning completely. The fact is, harmony has always been irrational. So its meaning has never been stable.

But back to the living – are the living composers who interest you the ones that are asking and answering similar questions to you, or the ones who are doing completely different things? Because I wouldn't say, for example, that Gerald Barry's music, with which you have a very close relationship, is so much involved in this kind of harmonic practice?

I was galvanised when I discovered Gerald's music. I think he really made a huge breakthrough and it was to do with his objective approach to material, something which I find very difficult, but very necessary. I heard his opera *The Triumph of Beauty and Deceit*. It seemed to me unprecedented: the combination of the ferociously objective treatment of the material and the intense passion of the working-out, and both at an extreme of brilliance. And the harmony – that there was harmony at all, and that it was so beautiful and lapidary. It functions, again, irrationally, but powerfully, to build tension and to create structure. It wasn't just repetitive. It builds. And the virtuosity, the display of it, that combination of things seemed, to me, to be new, and a major way forward.

In Barry it was all one moment of arrival after another, leading to another one. As someone who thinks transition-ally all the time and needs to work to find arrival points, I was fascinated by the way Barry could arrive abruptly just by, as it were, suddenly switching channels at the right moment – and it still felt achieved. I thought the effect was wonderful, so I wanted to see how it was obtained. I got very involved in *The Triumph* and even performed it many times.

Is this something you can learn? You described that as a way forward. Are you thinking of a way forward for you personally?

Of course.

And a way forward in general?

I can't speak for anybody else.

Is it related to your attraction to hard-edged writing? You've also talked about Janáček and Tchaikovsky in terms of the musical objects they create and that strikes me as not dissimilar to the way you think about Gerald Barry.

Artists are always attracted to do what they can't do easily. A challenge is always more interesting, because then you know you are making something, and not just doing whatever is automatic. I can see the effect of Gerald Barry on the first and second scenes of *The Tempest*, the first music with the singer, Miranda: she's looking out to sea and it's the aftermath of the storm and I created a texture that was new to me then, which is running quavers, but with a harmony. And I was excited because I felt there was actually a real counterpoint that would now be available, but a counterpoint that was not classical or baroque counterpoint, but something else – vertical harmony, but horizontally energised. It's very different, by the way, from what Barry does: endless canons, superimposition of canons and various other means. That wasn't what I was doing at all. But it was something to do with the three voices in a triad becoming – what's it called when you switch on an electric current? Animated? So they would be animated with a current that would lead through the triad. And I felt it was a way forward, because you then discover new relationships in those triads. But it doesn't sound like Barry at all, in practice.

And also the first scene, the storm. I'd written a long descriptive storm, with a build-up and a swell, almost all transition, towards one specific moment which I did very quickly when the storm breaks. And three years later I came back to it and I'd finished most of the opera and I realised it was unnecessary to have the build-up, because everyone knows there is going to be a storm, and there wasn't any point in sitting around for five minutes while it whipped itself up. I do have it whipping itself up for five seconds, because I think it wouldn't be truthful literally to start with a bang, as Verdi does in *Otello*, more or less, and which you can do in *The Tempest*. I've seen productions that start with a bang. But I thought, the storm is not the point; the point is the island, the fact that it's an island and that we want to get off it. The sea is there, and Prospero looks at it, and creates the storm with a geometry in his head. So I opened with a few seconds that show the sea, and then the storm comes immediately. So I threw away a great stack of material in that storm.

Actually threw away?

I burnt it in the sink.

Did you really do that?

I think so, yes. I normally would, things like that.

I'm thinking about smoke alarms.

I don't have smoke alarms. I hate them.

Objectivity: is there a danger of becoming too objective, of distancing yourself so much from your material that it loses the expressive power you want it to have?

I can only hope my safeguard against that is that I am very subjective. There's a subjectivity that happens when I pick up the pencil. That's why I feel I need that balance of forcing myself into a more objective relationship with the material. And I hope that would safeguard me from something that just becomes a mechanical manipulation.

Take the question of pattern. Music will have pattern in it, but the pattern is not the music. Pattern is essentially not alive, really, in the sense that DNA, or cells, or whatever, are not alive. They can be frozen. DNA has to be animated. There's always going to be a point with any artist where they say, 'I don't know why this works and this doesn't.' I think it's being conscious of pattern and also conscious of what is not pattern. Pattern is a very powerful thing, yet it mustn't be so powerful that it's the only thing in the music. That to me is boring.

You have shown me how some of the theoretical patterns and patterns in your music work: because the possibilities are infinite, can you imagine other composers using the same patterns to generate their music?

Of course. You would never know they were the same patterns, probably. It's all a process of genetic modification, really, what we do as composers. But that's only if it's done alertly. You must be alert, otherwise you will end up with something purely derivative.

Of course to make an imitation of an actual piece would

be pointless: 'He's done something that sounds like this. I want to do something that sounds the same.' This is exactly wrong. By all means use the material, but don't try and make it sound like mine. But that's probably the way these things normally do work. People try and make it sound like you and they get it wrong. That's very normal. It's one way to proceed.

Those patterns become a version of your kind of serialism – and yet serialism, the will to create pattern at all costs, and for that to be the most important thing in music, as it was for a period in the avant-garde, now seems a strange obsession for music to have had.

I think that was very much a thing that had to happen. You can so easily see it as a political metaphor: 'We need some order. Let's impose this.' And yet it doesn't have to be that. It had to be counteracted with another kind of madness, I think. I've actually become much more serial – certainly not in that kind of Schoenbergian sense, but when you're dealing with twelve notes and how they balance magnetically, serial thinking is at the end of that somewhere. But the idea of methodically going through from one to twelve and they're all equal: the problem with that approach is perhaps that there is no room for the possibility that they aren't equal.

But I do have a series in *In Seven Days*, the third movement, which is the organic flowering, the dry land and the trees, a spiralling series. It's a series that can be felt as counterpoint and harmony at the same time. It was an image for organic growth.

It's your way of ordering those twelve notes.

Yes. The twelfth is always the first of the next group, so it always modulates. And they always have suspensions. It is strict.

When you look back at your early music – because you're conscious now of all of those disciplines and orderings within your composition – do you see what you were doing then as more instinctive?

Yes and no. *Powder Her Face* is actually very strictly patterned. There's a lot of control. There's also a huge plunge into pillaging from all sorts of places, and the two apparently contradictory things are jammed together. Take the opening – I'd been playing around with a region of expanding harmonies and I heard a narrow sequence of two of them in a tango I was listening to, and the opening of that had one in it, so I took it.

And the tango was extremely helpful because expressively, it's precisely the right way to start that piece?

I don't know. It simply took me over. One doesn't plan these things.

So that tango is a quotation?

It's not just a quotation. Quotation is the wrong word. It's robbery.

Of a particular tune?

Yes. It's a Carlos Gardel tango. It's a very famous tune in Argentina. My Argentinian friend who came to the first performance of *Powder Her Face* said he nearly fell off his chair when he heard it. It's the most famous tune in Argentina. I didn't know. I only used the first few bars of it and then it goes on to something else. I just thought, 'This is going to open like this and sod it.' But its harmony informs much of the opera in a way that has absolutely nothing to do with that tune. The expanding harmony that I saw in the tango, I identified the inherent tendency in it; I took that as a cell and I put it in my own Petri dish and it ramified in all sorts of ways, which have absolutely nothing to do with that tango, those two chords. You take the two chords and you put them under a microscope and then you say, 'Actually, the cell's going this way,' and it goes in another direction.

What are the other bits of pilfery in it?

Oh, superficial things everywhere. Gewgaws. We've talked about that allusion to *The Rake's Progress*. Well, it continues into the next interlude, the graveyard scene, and then becomes Eugene Onegin. But a lot of the time they are fake quotations, red herrings, *pour tromper l'ennemi*. I wrote a whole song of my own in an absolutely straight-as-I-could-manage Jack Buchanan style. Some people would say, 'Why isn't it more satirical?' Because it's a gramophone record. Why would it be satirical, particularly? It's supposed to be a Twenties song, a Jack Buchanan song. A really specific thing. But it's as in a dream, a dream Jack Buchanan song, in which the intervals and the harmony behave according to my rules, so they're slightly off. But there is an illusion on the surface that it is the real thing. I was very pleased when my grandmother – who was probably biased, of course – said, 'It was exactly like the kind of music we used to have in those days at the Waldorf.' I thought it was very funny when critics said, 'Oh, Kurt Weill,' because there is really nothing to do with Weill, except the fact that there are saxophones playing. Proust said that critics remind him of film of early aviators, flapping their home-made wings impotently but never able to get more than a few inches off the ground.

You wrote that so quickly, that whole opera.

It didn't feel like it. It felt like pulling teeth.

Didn't you do it in seven months?

Something like that.

Do you have to go into a kind of trance to get those pieces written in that way?

No, you never sit down and think, 'I'm in a trance and here it comes.' It's working, working, working.

No, but I mean the work itself becomes so consuming that you're not completely in control of what's happening.

You can let the piece give you indications.

It's harder work that way.

Perhaps, because you're resisting a lot of the time. I can hear it in that piece. There's a terrific amount of resistance, of me kicking the material around. There may be an improvisatory feel to it, but in fact it's not at all improvisatory in structure. It's quite strictly regulated. One thing is that because of the nature of the subject – evanescence – the orchestration is very tenuous and risky; I think that's why I've come back to parts of the opera since then and put them in a more definite form.

There's something right at the start of The Tempest *that's common in so much of your music: the way you use extremes of register, the way a serene music in the highest possible register is blown off course by the gigantic violence in the bass register. You seem almost genetically attracted to those extremes, because they're in a lot of your pieces.*

Well, we have all the notes available; why would I not use the whole lot? They're just one end of the keyboard and another. The trouble is the extremes are more precarious and chancy instrumentally, including the bottom notes, but to me they're not extremes. I love that sound of the very highest octave, too, and I wish I was the kind of person who could truthfully write a whole piece that was only that sound. In *Tevot*, for example, there is one minute that is like that; I wish it was twenty. Maybe I will write a piece that's all up there. Unfortunately I've always got my eye somewhere else, looking at the horizon perhaps, so it goes down very quickly. It's a long process to reach stability.

But is there a difference between an F, say, up there, and one played in the middle of the orchestra? Are they completely different objects for you, different ideas, even if they are the same notes, just octaves apart and played on different instruments?

To me there's no distinction between colour and timbre and pitches. You can't just analyse something based on the pitches alone. You can't do it. It doesn't work in any period of music. You must say, 'This E flat at this pitch on the horn,' you must understand through the colour as well, or else it's meaningless. Anyone who's ever played a piano properly would understand that. Yes, you've got twelve notes, but it all hinges on where they are in the keyboard and how you balance them in chords, how loud you play one or the other, and how much pedal you use – these are integral parts of it. They are not separate things. The notes and the colour are inseparable, two sides of the same coin, and of equal value.

Orchestration is not an afterthought.

No, it's not. That's why it's entirely missing the point to say how wonderful Berlioz's orchestration is, because the point is, for Berlioz that particular major third on the clarinets has a particular quality, whereas if it was on an organ or on the flutes it would be a different, analytically different thing. It's not just colour. It's much more integral. I think people can often talk in a very uncomprehending way about orchestration and colour. It's not something that happens after the event.

So a lot of your orchestration is there immediately when you're writing a piece: it's not something that happens at a later stage.

It may be in the background. But yes.

Do things change in the course of orchestration?

Of course, it's molten all the time. Something that is a horn call for months, and then at the last minute you suddenly realise it has to be trombones or a harp. Yet it's still a horn call, expressively speaking, but one that is not played on horns. It has another function. That's very important, to allow that kind of shift to happen. Just as that horn call could be on the piano, a horn call in the orchestra can be on the piccolos.

Are the instruments ever articulating the drama? Or are they protagonists in it? Does instrumental colour become a kind of protagonist?

I think it's dangerous to get too dependent on just saying this character is represented by the trombone, and that one by the bassoon, because that's one-dimensional. In *The Tempest* I deliberately restricted the use of old-fashioned 'magical' sounds like glockenspiel or celeste. One has this choice, particularly dealing with a piece where the supernatural and magical qualities are one of the main subjects. Do we make the whole score actually full of vibraphones and waterphones? Well, maybe. I thought it better to create the impression that there were a lot of those colours, but in fact, use a strictly classical orchestra, really – and that would be the magic, until the feast scene late in Act III where

Prospero makes a false illusion appear. It's his big firework. His last big chance: he's going to take the entire court and completely trick them, and he makes the feast appear. And at that point I have somebody walk into the orchestra pit and play the harp for the duration of the scene and then walk out again, like in nineteenth-century opera. And the harpist finishes, plays a big arpeggio and walks out again. It's a conscious thing. So it's my way of saying: the magic side of it isn't really the point. We don't want to be all sitting there going, 'How magical this is,' because to me that's a too superficial response to the play.

Register is an issue in The Tempest *too, of course: I remember at the time you were composing it you were thinking about legibility and words – especially with the highest possible vocal tessitura you use for Ariel. That brings into focus your relationship with Shakespeare's words and Meredith Oakes's text in the opera.*

I saw that the text had to be, as it were, a translation of Shakespeare, that was at once modern and in some way suggestively archaistic. I knew Meredith's work through her libretto for Gerald Barry's *The Triumph of Beauty and Deceit* – and that she would certainly be the person to do this, because I wanted to approach Shakespeare as if foreign. Of course, we were writing the piece in Shakespeare's city, but the past is another country, so we should approach it like people living in another country and translate it, but in a translation that would be faithful to the spirit and the atmosphere of the original.

In fact it was a play I knew from early childhood. When you think of it you don't necessarily think of the specific words and speeches, but of the generalised atmosphere that this play produces. So we had to preserve that, but also make it functional for an operatic stage, which is a completely different beast from a theatrical stage. I could imagine all the composers who have thought about an opera on *The Tempest* thinking, 'I'll make an opera of *The Tempest*,' and sitting down to read the thing, and by the end of Scene 2 they're in despair because it is so apparently formless. Beethoven, Sibelius, Ligeti, et cetera. And opera is much more restrictive. Or I should say, the medium of opera demands more radical restrictions in order to work than that of spoken drama. So I wanted something that would make a geometry from the play, a more right-angled geometry, in two ways: firstly in the language itself, from line to line, and secondly in the plot. I felt, 'It won't work if we leave all these unconnected planes, these lacunae in the plot that Shakespeare has.' Things that don't really quite make sense, motives that don't quite add up, ends that are left untied, beautiful though they are. I knew omitting these things would leave one open to listeners saying, 'Well, it's not like Shakespeare.' Of course it's not. That's a play, this is not. I said, 'Firstly, do we want it to work or don't we?' And in order to work it would have to be translated in this way.

The three acts, the overall shape of the opera, those kind of things were your decision?

The music decided, really.

It wasn't that Meredith Oakes came up with the different versions that you approved or didn't approve?

We worked together on it, and also with the director, Tom Cairns. It had many versions. Until quite late on, the opera opened with Caliban saying, 'No such storm have I seen since my mother Sycorax was Queen,' the speech which is now in the middle of Act II after he sings, 'Friends don't fear.' So I did write all that first, which is why that music is everywhere all over the storm. Starting with Miranda was a much later idea.

Was the compositional process easier then, once the libretto had achieved its final form?

The libretto changed constantly as the music was written. I remember many difficult weeks of what felt like getting rid of pages and pages of musical material, and I cut away a lot of undergrowth all the time in the music. And this process would demand changes in the libretto too. At times I would tell Meredith I felt an obstacle and the music was not proceeding, and she would look at it and become aware that it was an occlusion of some kind in the libretto, perhaps a change of subject that was too sudden, and she would remove it and the music flowed on. The final lines of the chorus, 'Rejoice', for example, originally had a very different tone. It used to read 'From this point on / Everything will go just as smoothly.' And by that point in the opera such a tone was simply not available to me in the music, I had no way of doing it. So we changed it to 'You Gods look down / All who were lost are found.' By the time I got to Act III everything had to be boiled down to essentials. But you know, I think you find that in a lot of operas.

And in the end, there are just two or three lines of music, of material, almost throughout the opera.

That was the result of a huge amount of throwing away. I probably used the rubber more than I used the pencil in that piece. Often the simpler the piece, the longer you have to work.

The key at the end, D flat – you said it was unplanned, it came out of nowhere?

I don't know where it came from, really. It was there.

But one of the other really important centres in the piece is A major: there seems to be a connection between the A major music for Caliban and the stability that A major represents and embodies in your Piano Quintet – and in your orchestral pieces, too.

I never thought about it. It's at the end of *Tevot* and the end of *Polaris* too. The world is in A major. That's what I think. I think the earth revolves in A major, a low A.

Why?

Don't ask me. Ask a scientist.

It's not to do with 440 hertz that orchestras tune to, the oboe's A, because that's a cultural invention.

No, no, no. It's the low A, bottom A. Definitely.

That actual frequency?

I'm sure. I heard it. I think that's what the earth rotates at.

Have you heard it in nature anywhere, that sound?

I'm just conscious of it. I can hear it. These things all have a relationship. I mean C would be a human key, like the people's key, and A is the Earth.

Have you always known that?

After I wrote *The Tempest* I noticed it. I was just looking and I suddenly became aware of this unifying pitch.

So you don't hear it physically?

I hear it in my head, but it's when you have a view of a large part of the world or something, you can see it. I know it sounds ridiculous, but these things, they have to have a relation to each other like that: the earth, the sea, the sky, the human race, the animals, death, life, the cosmos, trees, plants; they have a relationship, and that can be expressed harmonically.

So what about the sea, then, does it have a fundamental tonal resonance too?

Well, the sea is many things, isn't it? The point is that the relations between these things can be expressed in notes. I've never written something that just describes the sea as a whole thing, because you can't do that; you're dealing with something that changes every second. But you can do seas of various kinds, harmonically. The opening of *The Tempest* is a seascape that somebody's looking at, that Prospero is looking at. So it's already a subjective seascape. And the storm is a geometrical storm created by him. It's not me looking at the sea and describing a nautical storm; it's a metaphorical storm. At the end of the opera, you have the sea and the island and the sky in harmony, but there is not one single element on its own that represents the sea. It's just there. I mean I've got a percussionist in the orchestra playing the geophone, an instrument that makes a noise like surf, because Caliban is actually sitting on the beach, listening to the sea, and it's not his subjective idea of the sea. It's the real sea, now. It's real nature, and it sounds like the sea. It's not really a metaphor any more. The metaphor is in the music: it's a metaphor of union, of equilibrium between the land and the air and the sea. You see, I have quite a geometrical way of thinking, after all.

9

finding Asyla *in Los Angeles –* Powder Her Face *and*
London *in the late 1990s – the other-worldly terrains of recent
pieces:* Tevot, *the Violin Concerto,* Polaris *– centrifugal
symphonies, Sibelius and Mahler – Brahms the symbolist –
composing operas on the ocean – opening doors*

*Your life is quite peripatetic. Does it affect your music? When
you write in one place, is it different from writing in another?*

Well, it affects the way one hears.

*That's a huge thing then: so you hear differently in this house in
London from how you do in Los Angeles?*

Yes, because the scale of sounds around you, the acoustic of
a sound in an emotional sense is so different, and the space
between one idea, one sound idea, and another varies
according to place, I find. Just as light is different or people
are different, so is sound. It won't necessarily affect what
goes down on the paper, but it won't necessarily not affect
it, because it affects the way things will sound next to each
other.

*You've talked about that passage in the Piano Quintet, where
you had a problem with the development section because you
were writing it in a place with trees outside. Are you any
happier working in and with nature now?*

164

No, it's still a distraction. I become more and more inspired by the natural world, but you don't have to be physically in it. Organic life: those things are not thinking about what they do – a flower doesn't decide to bloom, it just happens, or it doesn't; a tree doesn't decide to come into leaf, a bird doesn't decide to sing or migrate – it will just do something. That's ideally how it should be to work with musical material. But the human brain tends to create mayhem, and make things worse.

Are there other instances where pieces have been helped or hindered by the particular resonance of a place you're in, or your feeling of resonance with it?

When the conditions are more favourable you don't really notice. I think a view is unhelpful, usually, and too much space is unhelpful. But in a wider musical sense the moral construction, the moral build of places are different. So something may seem improper in one place, which is not at all problematic in another place, and vice versa. It's the same with things you say, which in one place can be considered outrageous or beyond the pale, and in another place quite normal. Think about politics: you can say something in Tel Aviv but if you said it in London it would be beyond the pale, and vice versa. The same thing goes in music, so you can say something in music in New York or in Los Angeles that you can't say in Berlin or London. It will have a different impact.

I see no harm in that, no reason not to avail myself of different spaces like that. I mean I don't sit down and think, now I'm in America I can write this note rather than that note, it's not quite as banal as that. It's more a general sense of another dimension, which can make itself felt as a kind of freedom. I mean it could certainly work in the other direction: an American-born composer could come and live in Europe and suddenly feel themselves freer. That's quite possible. It depends where one starts, but the point is it's a change, a stretch to one's musical body that allows one to reach further.

What was the first piece you wrote in America?

The first time I wrote any music in America would have been in 1996, when I first went to Los Angeles. And I was halfway through writing *Asyla*. I'd already written the first two movements in a form that was fairly close to that of the finished piece. I was aware that the third movement needed to be a kind of dance movement, and I also had an idea that it might take place in some modern context, but I wasn't quite sure. I had a fairly good idea but I just didn't know how to realise it. And then I sat down in Los Angeles, in a windowless room in the Dorothy Chandler Pavilion – this is before Frank Gehry's Disney Hall was built. And I had a very simple breakthrough, to do with the repetition. I knew some repetition would have to be involved and it was a question of dealing with the repetition without the repetition becoming the point. I've no idea whether I succeeded – some would certainly say I hadn't.

I realised it wasn't enough to just repeat two or three or four times, I had to think in terms of thirty-two, sixty-four times to achieve what I wanted. And then there was the question: is it literal repetition or was the colour of the thing going to shift, and what were the shifts going to be? And in two or three sittings I had the whole thing sketched in Los Angeles. I don't know whether that would have happened here at home in London. I did much of the detail in London, but I was definitely conscious of an opening up of a new landscape over there.

But you were sitting in a windowless room in a concert hall – there was no landscape you could see, that your eye could be drawn to.

Well, obviously I'm not talking about a physical landscape in that literal sense – and that would have been a distraction, like the trees! But I was aware that outside was a world that was completely different to anywhere I'd been.

What were you doing there?

I'd been invited to take part in a concert with the Los Angeles Philharmonic, their new-music strand of concerts, the Green Umbrella Series. I played the piano. Everything about the place felt alien in an exciting way.

It wasn't your first time in America?

No, I'd been to New York, and to northern California too, but of course downtown LA at that time was not like any city centre I'd ever been in before. You were told not to go one block away from the concert hall. It's changed a lot now, for the better. I had to go and find a pencil sharpener because in those days I hadn't yet discovered the rotating pencil – which is now the secret of life to me. I was still sharpening my pencils, then, and in LA you couldn't just go to the newsagent and buy a pencil sharpener. The word 'newsagent' means nothing, there's no such thing: you say the word 'newsagent' to them and they'd imagine some character from Raymond Chandler phoning a story through. And certainly there aren't corner shops. In a way, there aren't really corners, either, not in the way we have them here. Not for pedestrians. And in the course of trying to find a pencil sharpener I went down one block and I was suddenly in another century, it felt like, another world, another language. It was dramatic. I just felt immediately I'd set off on some wider journey. And I think I became able to realise what I wanted with less self-consciousness, I suppose. Who knows, maybe it would have happened if I'd gone and done it in Burma, I don't know.

It's the being away from home, being elsewhere, that was the important creative freedom for you?

I didn't want the music to have a sense of freedom, particularly: the music could sound as free or constricted as it liked. I don't hold with this idea of loosening up. It's not as simple as that. In some ways going to LA actually allowed me to be more focused, but it's more that I felt freer to make certain choices in the piece, to do what had to be done to get to the end, to get out of the piece.

Have you written pieces anywhere apart from America and England?

I composed a cello and piano piece recently, a lot of which was written in Zürich, and including a whole section which I see as nude mountaineering ladies, the trio of a movement called 'La Montagne'. I think of it as a very Swiss piece, a very Zürich piece specifically. Zürich feels like a city that's only there for the convenience of the Swiss, because they like to come down from the mountains and do business and then disappear into the mountains again. So it's a kind of invisible city, like LA. It's got an element of the Alpine air about it, I suppose. But again I was in a little room with no view, it's not as if I had a panorama of the lake or anything.

You're obviously comfortable as a human being and a musician in LA's invisible city: you've made an identity there in all sorts of ways, partly because you've performed a lot there and elsewhere in America. You've performed a lot in New York, as a conductor, as a solo pianist at Carnegie Hall, and The Tempest *is being produced at the Met. In fact, you probably perform more in America than you do here, especially your orchestral music. Do you feel more comfortable there?*

In Britain there is more of a dissonance, perhaps because there are expectations, others can wrongly consider themselves directly involved in your development and get very bossy. And of course the only person involved in my development is me. In the States I feel there is an infinite horizon and one could pick a goal at any point along it.

As a composer or a conductor?

Everything. I'm an animal that does what it does. I'm afraid I can't change anything about myself because somebody else has had a difficult day. That can be a problem, particularly in your own country where everybody has their nose in each other's business. There can be some huge misunderstandings, like the absurdity of anybody writing that one could be the next Benjamin Britten, as they did at the beginning of my career. I mean once you remove the intended compliment, which is questionable anyway, it's just so absurd, because why should that be the thing anyone would want to do in 1990? It doesn't make any sense. It's just so unhelpful and confusing: it's a different time, can't we just look at each other as what we actually are, rather than what we're not, and not even trying to be? You can rub along with this sort of thing and even play along with it for a bit, but then suddenly you realise this is a complete distraction, it's a Boojum. And maybe it's better to just go. Especially when we're not starting from the same standpoint at all, there's no need to be on the same land mass.

It strikes me that your life in Los Angeles, the way you described that ability to be more comfortable there, is not unlike the way that you've described the sense of place in your pieces, and the realm of idealised escape and elsewhere that they represent. There's a connection there.

It's possible. In some ways the distractions of place can be beneficial. *Powder Her Face* is very much set in London and I think you can hear that atmosphere of the late Nineties. It was a very explosive place at that time, in a way very decadent, the crumbling city and the dissonance between the established London culture and the new, rougher one. And in some ways there was a sense of the barbarians taking over, and it was very exciting. It reminded me of something I saw around the same time, thousands of monkeys jumping over a pyramid in Central America. I hear all that in the piece, it's an extremely London piece. I even hear the Park Lane traffic in it.

But then you start to think, well, that's just one piece, that's a very isolated piece – and there have to be other places. And to me *Asyla* is another piece about place, but it's beginning to move away from London. It's more about turning away. It's nothing very mysterious, but I just happen to like it, those different lights and spaces. So there is some relation between the place and the music, but it's not absolute.

I have to do a lot of tuning it out. I am rather like a radio, and London was in a way like a kind of pirate radio station that would suddenly start broadcasting on my channel. I thought it would be interesting to see what happened if we took London out of the equation for a bit. Maybe going somewhere else is a way of finding out what's in my head. But you can't be definitive about these things.

You have said each piece has a locus, each work ought to have a specific metaphorical place it occupies.

A locust?

A locus. Something, some specific terrain.

Oh, location.

It seems to my ears that the terrain of a lot of your pieces is becoming increasingly wide and more cosmic; the spaces they define are getting bigger and bigger. I'm thinking of The Four Quarters, In Seven Days, Polaris, Tevot, *the Violin Concerto.*

I can't tell. It might be true.

It does sound like that to me. Maybe the way to put it is that the spaces your music creates are defined by a sense of there being something huge just at the borders that's suggested by the material in the piece. So the music we're hearing in those pieces is a suggestion of some space or dimension that is much bigger than the time and space the pieces actually occupy. Paradoxically, magically, they are definitively in a particular space, but they are also giving you visions of this huge universe beyond their borders.

I'm aware that, increasingly, my thinking is centrifugal – when you think from a point and everything is spun outwards – rather than centripetal. I recognise this, too, in some symphonists that I really like. It's interesting if you look at the difference between someone like Sibelius and someone like Mahler. In a symphony you're supposed to create something that closes a circle. Sibelius symphonies are fascinating because I think they come from a conflict between the symphonic impulse to bring things round full circle, and an inner desire to go off into an endless horizon of trees or lakes or pure song or whatever it is – the undiscovered country. I think that's what the material wants to do, but he can't let it, because he has to make it symphonic. The conflict becomes more and more powerful as the symphonies go on. In the Fifth it is a huge struggle which is achieved, in the Sixth it seems so powerful that it has to happen just offstage, and in the Seventh there is a sense that although he makes it in the end he is all but broken by the effort. It becomes an increasingly agonising process. But in the tone poems, he is released from the conflict of having to make an abstract argument that functions logically. So the end of *Tapiola* is deeply conclusive, but the end of the Seventh Symphony is painfully inconclusive.

Your recent music seems more deeply conclusive, in that sense.

Well, I couldn't compare. But *Polaris*, for example, is very simple, it's a much simpler structure than *Tevot*, and it does have a beginning, a middle and an end, clearly functioning as those three things. And yet still I had to end *Polaris* with a complete splaying, an explosion, of its material.

Do you mean that the simplicity of the structure of pieces like Polaris *means that they are more spherical objects, more complete?*

I'm saying that with Sibelius, the function of symphonic completeness passed from the 'abstract' into the 'metaphorical', and I think it has stayed there. I think he was the first to break, painfully, the mistaken idea that a symphonic argument had to have a sort of structural order to it. There's a big problem with the word 'symphony', because I think it's expected that it should be something with a certain inevitable kind of structure or decorum to it. But that was never the case. That was always a mistake.

What about Brahms, in those terms?

Well, that's a bad case, a tragic sham.

All four of his symphonies?

I love the Third Symphony, it's beautiful, but it's a symbolist work masquerading as a symphony. He's a symbolist composer in every way, masquerading as a symphonist. The real Brahms is in the *Alto Rhapsody*, *Song of Destiny*, those beautiful songs: they're wonderful, troubling, strange, shadowy things. But the moment he forces himself to put on a black tie and write a concert symphony, to me it just stinks of fake, phoniness, in the way of course Beethoven never possibly can – or very rarely. Brahms is a big passionate country symbolist peasant dreamer and poet, a huge natural musical creature, who's forcing himself to put on urban clothes, a bow-tie because he thinks that to write a symphony, you have to dress up in your best town clothes. And he is wrong.

But what about the finale of the Fourth Symphony?

It's a terrible waste of space.

But surely it's all about closing the circle, creating a spherical kind of completeness through the single-minded power of that passacaglia?

It's full of holes.

Where?

There's a huge hole just before the end. The piece stops and then starts again. It's not well done at all, he should have had another go. It's not convincing. It's as untrue as when people say *The Turn of the Screw* is very formal because it happens to be quasi-serial. They are gullibly following cues the composers left them, like lemmings, like sheep. Brahms is not at all the composer he's pretending to be. That piece is not a successful passacaglia.

Well, by most people's standards it is.

I don't care. It's not.

The late piano pieces?

Maybe, they're so floral and symbolic. I mean I don't like all of them, there's some of them that are a little bit industrial. You can hear the pistons going in them. They often use exactly the same material at different speeds, but it behaves the same way.

As opposed to the material being on its own terms, allowed to do what it wants?

Well, you're actually too aware of the material, you're too aware that Brahms is playing around with bits of material. They're largely just the same thing in different moods, those pieces. But then he will discover something that changes the game completely, with no apparent effort, because one must always remember he had a great natural genius for the mechanics of music. But with Chopin, say, you never listen to Chopin and think it's thirds, it's fifths: it's far beyond; you're floating in space.

So it's the playing around, not the material, that's the problem for you?

It's a little bit amateurish.

And Beethoven – who also plays around with material, after all?

You're not even aware in Beethoven that you're dealing with such and such a motive, these things are far beneath him. But in Brahms, there's often a sense of duty that spoils the effect. When he's just playing around with imagery and pleasing himself, and not forcing it into a concert shape, but letting it go where it wants to, I find it much more successful, as in the *Song of the Fates*.

Has it become harder to find a musical world that can become another opera? Because in instrumental music, it's fine to have that suggestion of a perspective on something much bigger, some ocean beyond the concerto, or the orchestral piece. But in opera – for your third opera, on Buñuel's The Exterminating Angel *– haven't you got to try and find lots of islands of material, to locate the drama and the characters, as opposed to suggestions of the infinite?*

Well, how are you going to find islands unless you are at sea? I hope so. I'm hoping so, I've had breakthroughs in the past with this and I'm hoping I'll have another one this time.

But is that the essence of what the challenge is going to be?

I don't know what's going to happen until I start putting the first things down, or why it is that certain landscapes are conjured – why, when I put three or four notes down, a certain landscape is suggested to me, and a certain way of continuing. I just allow it.

It's just that I can imagine a symphony set out on that musical ocean, or a four-and-a-half-hour-long orchestral piece projected onto the waves, but does it become more difficult when you have to put people somewhere on that sea?

Well, the people in the film of *The Exterminating Angel* are on the Raft of the *Medusa*. One of its early inspirations was a play called *The Shipwrecked*. They're prevaricating so hard that they can't move out of this room even though its doors are open. It's territory that I like very much, because it looks as though they're in a room, but it's not really about the room, they're actually trapped in their own heads.

As in The Tempest *or* Powder Her Face *or* Asyla.

Well, yes, why don't we just go through the door?

I wonder: what would happen if you went through all the doors you had available to you, all those doors into the infinite that you have discovered in your music?

Well, you can't, you have to open them one by one – you can't just go round opening all the doors. Think of Alice. You might have to go back to the table and eat some of the cake or drink some of the drink to be the right size.

You've used the metaphor of doors throughout these conversations: going through another door then another door . . .

. . . into the rose garden. That's Eliot.

Is that where it comes from, the doors?

No, it's just a wonderful passage in *Four Quartets* which I love very much. But yes, I do think that's what one's experience is.

Opening doors, finding other spaces, elsewheres from where you are?

A thing becomes possible which makes another thing possible which wouldn't have been possible without it. That's life. I mean, you can just barge through a door; but I can imagine barging through a door and not knowing what to say, and whatever's behind it just looking at you in puzzlement. You have to enter and understand. That's what is happening to me all the time, continually being released from one space into another, finding what's behind the door, and emerging, again, into another elsewhere.

List of Works

The Lover in Winter (1989)
four songs for countertenor and piano

Five Eliot Landscapes Op. 1 (1990)
soprano and piano

Chamber Symphony Op. 2 (1990)
chamber ensemble of fifteen players

O thou who didst with pitfall and with gin Op. 3a (1990)
anthem for male voices

Gefriolsae me Op. 3b (1990)
anthem for male voices and organ

Catch Op. 4 (1991)
chamber ensemble of four players

Darknesse Visible (1992)
piano solo

Fool's Rhymes Op. 5 (1992)
SATB chorus and ensemble

Under Hamelin Hill Op. 6 (1992)
chamber organ (one to three players)

Still Sorrowing Op. 7 (1992)
piano solo

Life Story Op. 8 (1993)
soprano and chamber ensemble of three players

Living Toys Op. 9 (1993)
chamber ensemble of fourteen players

. . . but all shall be well Op. 10 (1993)
orchestra (also version for reduced orchestra)

Sonata da caccia Op. 11 (1993)
chamber ensemble of three players

Arcadiana Op. 12 (1994)
string quartet

Les Baricades mistérieuses (1994)
arrangement of Couperin for chamber ensemble of five
players

Life Story Op. 8a (1994)
soprano and piano

The Origin of the Harp Op. 13 (1994)
chamber ensemble of ten players

Cardiac Arrest (1995)
arrangement of Madness for chamber ensemble of seven
players

Powder Her Face Op. 14 (1995)
chamber opera in two acts and eight scenes for four singers
and fifteen players

Traced Overhead Op. 15 (1996)
piano solo

These Premises Are Alarmed Op. 16 (1996)
orchestra

Asyla Op. 17 (1997)
large orchestra

Concerto conciso Op. 18 (1997)
piano and chamber ensemble of ten players

The Fayrfax Carol (1997)
SATB chorus (divisi) with optional organ

America – A Prophecy Op. 19 (1999)
mezzo-soprano and large orchestra with optional large
chorus

January Writ (1999)
SATB chorus (divisi) and organ

Piano Quintet Op. 20 (2000)

Brahms Op. 21 (2001)
baritone and orchestra

The Tempest Op. 22 (2003)
opera in 3 acts

Court Studies from *The Tempest* (2005)
clarinet, violin, cello and piano

Concerto for Violin – *Concentric Paths* Op. 23 (2005)
violin and chamber orchestra

Three Studies from Couperin (2006)
chamber orchestra

Dances from *Powder Her Face* (2007)
orchestra

Tevot Op. 24 (2007)
orchestra

In Seven Days Op. 25 (2008)
piano and orchestra with moving image

Concert Paraphrase on *Powder Her Face* (2009)
piano

Lieux retrouvés Op. 26 (2009)
cello and piano

Mazurkas Op. 27 (2009)
piano

The Four Quarters Op. 28 (2010)
string quartet

Polaris Op. 29 (2012)
voyage for orchestra

Index

183